THIRD EYE ACTIVATION MASTERY

Proven And Fast Working Techniques To Increase Awareness And Consciousness

L. Jordan

5th Edition

Free gift inside this book

Table of Contents

Introduction

Chances are you have heard of the Third Eye. Most people have. Unfortunately, the third eye most people know is possibly the investigative eye; someone you hire to check out who could be sabotaging your business, your relationship, and such. Investigative firms, for example, might view themselves as their clients' third eye. However, the third eye discussed in this book relates to the power of vision that you gain when you learn how to exercise some out-of-the-body discipline.

In this book, you can learn more about the basics of opening the third eye. You will learn the simple things that you need to do on a regular basis, but which have enormous rewards in terms of being aware of what is happening around you. Once you have learnt how to open your third eye, you will be able to tell when you are in a hostile environment and when you are in a friendly environment. Whichever happens to be the case, you then can make a move that best suits your circumstances. Being able to open your third eye also gives you a quick and easy avenue to relax both your mind and your body, something that leaves you well placed to make objective decisions in whatever you are doing.

For your information, some people have their third eye open right from birth, in fact so open that they pass as natural psychics. This book will help you see if you a natural psychic or not, or if someone close to you happens to be. This is important because some parents who have children with psychic abilities tend to think those children are mentally unstable. And that goes too for the abilities of a medium – the one with an even higher level of intuition and vision, and which happens to take a much more spiritual dimension. You will read all about the distinguishing features between a psychic and a medium in this book. Hence, you will be able to understand yourself when you feel like you are thinking out of this world, and others too when other people may see them as weirdoes.

Incidentally, when it comes to the opening of your third eye, at times it just inadvertently flips open. You will read about that in this book and see how you can be so ordinary one day and the next you are all visual and prophetic. In fact, that is how the world has gotten some of its most famous mediums – in a very abrupt and unplanned way. However, as already mentioned, there are the natural born psychics as you will clearly see in this book. And whichever way each of the psychics gets their third eye open, the fact is that they all have very high level of intuition that any person would benefit from.

It is worth a mention that even as you have your third eye open, there is need for you to keep stimulating it. Failure to do that coupled with the fact that there is plenty of negative energy in our environment can lead to it being dormant and thus unhelpful. In this book you will see how to keep your third eye activated and also how to prevent it from getting somewhat blocked.

This book also teaches you how to close your third eye. It shows you why opening your third eye can sometimes be overwhelming, and it teaches you how to remedy the situation in such instances. From this book, you get to learn that the skills of opening and closing your third eye are not just useful to monks and other religious figures, but they are also useful to ordinary people.

The future for you is waiting to be uncovered. If you are ready to get more intuitive, you need to read this book and put into practice the simple lessons given. You will realize that there is nothing necessarily religious about meditation, yet it can go a long way to opening your higher understanding of happenings in your life. You will be in a position to psych yourself for certain eventualities that you may sense during the period your third eye is highly energized.

And if you end up being a psychic medium, you will be able to help many people to pass on personal heartfelt messages to their loved ones who may have passed on and left them with lots of questions and great amount of anxiety. On the converse, you will also be able to communicate messages from the spirits to living persons and thereby setting those spirits free to proceed to their resting place instead of dwelling on the plane between the physical world and the spiritual world. Plainly speaking, as a psychic medium, you will be very valuable to both the living and the spirits of the dead.

In matters of intuition and psychic competence, this book offers just the solution you have been looking for. In fact, you could even make a fortune from your unique abilities as a medium or even for being able to make astral travels that can be of interest to certain individuals.

Happy reading and best wishes in activating your third eye

Chapter 1:
What, Exactly, Is The Third Eye?

How many eyes do you normally have? Well, you, obviously, know of two; the physical ones that are conspicuous and clearly located within your face. But there are, very likely, times that you see something for the first time, yet you have this feeling that it is not exactly new. Chances are that you had visualized whatever it is you are seeing now, but at a sub-conscious level. And much as we may be using *sub-conscious* here, in certain disciplines, it comes across as a level of, say – higher consciousness. At certain times too, you have this strong feeling about something and you may reckon it is your mind directing your line and density of thought, yet it happens to be a function of your third eye. So you cannot wonder that it is sometimes referred to as your mind's eye.

Has the third eye always existed?

From the old school of thought, the third eye has a lot to do with the mystical – some extraordinary ability to perceive things you cannot see with your naked eyes. In fact, in many cases, it is seen as ability to perceive things even before they happen; the reason the third eye is sometimes referred to as the speculative and invisible eye. Of course, since it is not visible it is also termed the inner eye. And, in a somewhat amusing way, in some faiths, it is even given a location. In Hinduism, for example, it is said to be on your brow – right between your eyebrows, but slightly above the eyebrow junction. You have possibly seen members of the Hindu community wear a red mark right on that spot.

In theosophy, which is a study of the divine within the Greek philosophy, the third eye is considered as being located within the pineal gland. This is a serious subject but it is sprinkled with funny aspects. When it comes to this discipline that is theosophy, for instance, it is believed that once upon a time – sounds like a tale of the ogres – the human third eye used to be physically located right at the back of your head (oops!). Sure – and it did perform both the physical role of watching and also the spiritual role of seeing the invisible.

Then, what the heck happened?

Well, ever heard that once upon a time you were monkeys? And then you learnt how to walk on twos and your brain developed somewhat and you became the bright beings that you are today? That is called evolving. And so, apparently, you may have had that physical third eye in those early stages of development, and it sort of dissolved or disappeared into your cranium (too much imagination here...), and now what you are left with is the ability to sense out-of-body things from your pineal gland.

Scientific perspective to the third eye

Incidentally, some highly educated people seem to see a lot of sense in the third eye and are trying to understand its mode of operation better. There is this doctor of psychiatry, Dr. Rick Strassman, who tends to see some link between the pineal gland and the excretion of the chemical, entheogen. Entheogen, for your information is said to induce different states of consciousness. So you see – the existence of the third eye is not a matter of mythical stories; religious hypnosis and fanaticism; or such other not-easy-to-believe practices. It is some reality that you may wish to appreciate; acknowledge, and even make use of.

And what is the modern sense of the third eye?

In the present day, the third eye does not change its basics since it is still invisible and not necessarily easy to comprehend; but it is associated more with enlightenment of sorts. It is also associated with your ability to understand and make best use of your chakras – those nerve centers that exist in different parts of your body, and which have a lot to do with your emotional, psychological and spiritual welfare.

In a religious sense, the third eye has got a lot to do with visions. In this respect, people who make good use of their third eye are often believed to be seers. On the overall, the third eye has plenty to do with non-physical experiences as well as precognition.

How, for the love of mystery and wit, do I begin to comprehend the third eye?

Yeah – if you are not into chakras and visions, you may be wondering what will make you understand the third eye better. Here is a case that will ring a bell:

Supposing your friend is grieving and you find that whatever words you prepare to say as a show of solidarity are not sufficient. Just being around this friend and showing empathy does wonders; your friend understands that you are communicating empathy and solidarity. You know what you are effectively doing in this case? You are utilizing the power of the third eye to send your heartfelt emotions to that person. The truth is that you and everyone else have the third eye. And evidently, your third eye does not just receive information, it also transmits it.

Another way of looking at the third eye

You know what a student portal is, don't you? The site where you log into and access whatever that appertains to you as a student – a place that is highly concentrated with information useful to you in particular and not the entire institution in general. That is precisely what your third eye is like – a portal that is concentrated with such great and positive energy, that it is able to sharpen your thinking and direct your focus. As such you find yourself with a high level of intuition; imagination; creativity; and also wisdom. And you can now see how you get to the high level of consciousness.

Does the third eye make you a psychic?

It is said that some people have their third eye open in a natural way, but you can also make a deliberate move to have your third eye open. Those people with their third eye very wide open from birth and they are aware of it are the ones you consider psychic. In their lot are some, in fact, who have been relied upon to help in criminal investigations because the energies of their third eye direct their focus on where the action is even without their physical presence.

Of course opening your third eye is not necessarily going to produce a psychic out of you, but you will, definitely, be more aware of your environment – the positive and negative energy within it – and even be realistic about the possibilities of certain eventualities.

Chapter 2:
The Fascinating History of the Third Eye

History can be strange, can't it? Bringing unimaginable realities to the fore, like the fact that this decently dressed human race that lives in decent buildings today once strolled the open lands all nude and retreated into their dwelling caves when the day was done. And, of course, that was after some great evolvement from walking on all fours – good gracious! Gladly, it now looks like the evolvement – at least the physical aspect of it – is over.

Other living things have their history too. And when you look at this third eye that is usually taken as having its physical form in the pineal gland, it is symbolized by the pine cone. For one, both have been in existent for as long as you would not care to remember. As has been mentioned earlier, the pineal gland existed even in the more crude forms of the human being. And if you think that natural vegetation has always been as you see it today, forget it.

There was an era when the earth had no flowers. How ugly! Yet the Pine Cone tree was still standing tall on the earth. In fact, it is said that flowering plants have only existed for a third of the Pine Cone tree's lifetime. Of course, the similarity between the pineal gland and the pine goes further to incorporate both the shape of the cone and that of the pineal gland. As the spines of the cone spiral in all directions in a kind of Fibonacci sequence, your pineal gland sits geometrically right in the middle of your brain.

At the same time this gland has a lot to do with the amount of light being processed and absorbed into your body from all dimensions as well as its intensity. No wonder it determines your sleep and waking patterns through this role of light transduction. Of great significance is its centrality when it comes to your overall enlightenment.

When did the appreciation of the pineal gland as the third eye begin?

This can only be said to be as old as the human consciousness of themselves. The Egyptians, the Assyrians, the Indians, the Greeks, the Romans, religious and non-religious people, all have had some exaltation for the third eye, and always relating it to the physical location of the pineal gland.

Visualize this example of the Egyptians who as long ago as 1224BC have depicted the staff of their god, Osiris, as two serpents rising up in an intertwined form until they find themselves at a pinecone. Compare that then with its parallel in the Indian culture. There when you are at your pinnacle of enlightenment your Kundalini is deemed to be fully activated – Kundalini, of course, being that spiritual energy within your body. At that point in time, all your chakras are considered to be in proper alignment and well coordinated.

How do the Indians depict this highest level of spiritual awareness? Likewise, they show that as serpents coiling up from the bottom of your spine to the location of your pineal gland; thus connecting with your third eye. According to the Indians, you must reach this level of spiritual awareness to be able to attain Divine wisdom – the moment of experiencing nothing but joy, knowledge, love; all in their purest form.

And how did the Assyrians take the pinecone? Actually, it was more than a symbol of enlightenment; also signifying immortality. This is clear from their carvings that are said to have existed somewhere between 713 and 716 BC. Those carvings show godlike figures each with four wings, and holding out pinecones. And they are not just holding the pinecones but actually pollinating some symbolic Tree of Life.

In the Hindu belief, this connection of the divine and the cone continues to be seen as Shiva, the most revered of the Hindu gods, is drawn, sculpted or even carved into an image with an outstretched hand holding a pinecone. Often, the image of the god even shows the hair coiled and shaped into a form of cone, often with a serpent or more interwoven within it.

And the Mexicans are in it too; taking the pinecone as being symbolic of high spiritual awareness as well as immortality. They depict their god named Chicomecoat, meaning Seven Snakes, in the act of giving out pinecones using one hand, and with the other hand holding out an evergreen tree.

And for the Greeks as well as the Romans, that god Dionysus who comes with religious ecstasy and fertility, and whose reference later changed to Bacchus, is commonly shown carrying a fennel staff which, while woven with the climbing plant, Ivy, ends up being capped at the top with a pinecone. That staff goes by the name, Thyrsus, and is said to be all drippy with honey. It is held sacred and is used exclusively for rituals and fetes associated with religion.

In fact, there is even this gigantic sculpture made of bronze, which the Romans put up three stories high, and it happens to be pine shaped. It is believed to have served as a huge water fountain located near the Temple of Isis. Incidentally, Isis was the goddess, wife of god Osiris. All that legendary activity was in ancient Rome, yet the structure still stands today but within the *Court of the Pinecone* before the Vatican. And Vatican being the headquarters of the Catholic faith, the continued

14

existence of that sculpture is indication that the religion is not also averse to the whole association with the pinecone.

In fact, there is a marked occurrence of items of pinecone shape within the Catholic faith. Of great significance is the Pope's sacred staff whose tip is shaped like a pinecone. The shape is also notable on the Vatican flag right within the Coat of Arms where you find three crowns shaped like pinecones. Once inside a Catholic church, there is a high chance you are going to identify something in the shape of a pinecone. Particularly you may find candle holders and even lamps. And with these lighting items with their obvious illumination, you can make a plausible link parallel to the third eye.

In addition, think of the Pope's reference as Holy See. You can easily reference that to the third eye, which is understandable considering that the Pope is considered to be very close to the Divine; a revered person who issues orders on matters spiritual with unquestionable authority.

Chapter 3:
A Good Range of Implementable Psychic Abilities

It is invisible alright, this third eye, but it sure allows you to see verifiable things and scenarios. That is what makes working with the third eye so fascinating. Has he been away for two years and all of a sudden his live image has emerged before you? And you may probably be thinking – where on earth has this image emerged from and I have not spoken to him for months? Then you hear a knock and casually go for the door. And who appears before your naked eyes? Him! Just a while ago you saw his image – now here he is in person. That now is psychic; or what we often refer to as:

The 6th sense – that extra sensory perception (ESP) that leads you to receiving information without physical intervention. It is a state of heightened sensory awareness.

Other psychic abilities include:

Telepathy

Here your mind sort of communicates with that of another person and you are able to tell what the other person is feeling even when you are both a whole distance apart.

Clairaudience

Have you heard of prophets who heard the voice of God and went ahead to convey the message to nations far away from where they had heard the voice? This is the kind of stuff clairvoyance is made of – hearing inaudible voices, that is, sensible sounds right within your mind; or even audible voices.

Clairvoyance

This is your psychic ability to visualize images, pictures or impressions, which you can relate to your environment or to reality, whether physically around you or far from you. You usually see such images through your third eye. By the way, this terminology is derived from French where it carries the meaning of 'clear seeing'.

Clairsentience

This is that ability to be empathetic to other people. Have you come across certain people you feel so good being around particularly when you are feeling low? Somehow they seem to emit that aura of 'everything is going to be alright' and you feel it and you absorb it. Such people are simply able to transmit their empathy to you psychically.

Dowsing

Have you ever misplaced something yet you were so sure it was still in the house? Here is where dowsing comes in, and it is the use of something like a pendulum to help you locate it. What you do here is concentrate on sensing your energy flow as you pose the question regarding the position of your misplaced item. Dowsing tools usually come in shapes of L or even Y; and you can make your own from a coat hanger. You could also use a fishing rod as your dowsing tool or even a self-made pendulum.

Channeling

This is some psychic ability that makes you act as a medium. What this essentially means is that you can have the ability to receive messages from some spiritual power, which you are then supposed to deliver to someone in person. And when you are not delivering such messages, you are possibly causing things that are beyond an ordinary person to happen; what we would call paranormal activities.

Automatic writing

When you possess the psychic power of automatic writing, you can find yourself practically writing things down that are being communicated to you by a superior spiritual being; things that are not of your own making. In this instant, you are clearly acting as a trance medium. Often too, you can find yourself unblocking your creative edge in a way you never knew possible.

Medical intuition

When you have this psychic ability, you are able to tell what elements in your environment can be useful in physical healing and even which ones you can combine to create a healing product. It is like you have an innate gift of recognizing items with medicinal properties.

Medium

As a medium, you have the psychic ability to communicate with the spirits of people who are departed; yet you are alive. Such spirits can direct you to where their bodies are if they are at large, the reason mediums often become useful in criminal investigations.

Psychometric ability

You can use this psychic ability to tap crucial information from a mere photograph or such other objects.

Readers

Often you come across readers who have psychic abilities. Such readers include Palm Readers.

Scrying

This psychic ability involves being able to foretell an outcome by looking at a shiny surface – a crystal ball; a mirror; a bowl of water; or any other such glossy surface.

Remote viewing

This is the psychic ability that enables you to have some astral projection – being able to traverse long distances and seeing vividly whatever is happening there, without moving your physical body an inch. You can do that within a couple of minutes and when you resume your normal existence you make a call and confirm that what you saw in your spiritual travel was actually true. Sometimes you may not even make a call – you could simply hear an announcement on Cable News and confirm that what you had seen psychically was reality

Chapter 4:
How Do You Open That Third Eye?

Is there really only one way to skin a – no; you do not want trouble with animal activists so you dare not see yourself skinning a cat, whichever eye you are using. So let us ask, is there just one way of catching a thief? And the answer is no – there are more than one way. You could lie in wait; set up CCTV cameras; and many other ways. Likewise, there is more than one way to open your third eye. You could do this and do that; but ultimately the practice you put into the whole experience is what determines how successfully you manage to open that third eye.

Meditation

In meditation, you seek out some quiet place. And do not worry; we appreciate the world is one noisy place. So your place need not be as quiet as a deserted church – just quiet enough to let you focus without major distractions. Again, it needs to be a place where you can sit down. This is how you go about it:

- Sit right on the floor. Whether you have laid a mat or not is not consequential.

- Set up your back; it needs to be straight

- Cross your legs before you – well, you cannot really cross them any different way, can you?

- Rest your open hands on your knees

- You are now set for meditation…

Hold on! Suppose sitting on the floor is a no for me? That is a question you should expect from many people, but the truth is – that is not a reason for you or anyone else to let meditation pass. So, in case, for some reason you cannot actually sit on the floor, or possibly you do not want to, get a chair and sit on it. Just ensure that your back remains straight.

And how is the rest of the body in the meantime? Well:

- Chest – out

- Abdominal muscles – tight

What is the big deal with abdominal muscles? Well, they are very important in supporting the upper part of your body.

- And shoulders – down

Why down for the shoulders? Well, you are required to relax; that is the reason. In fact, you need to consciously let your body go even as you observe the areas pointed out above, of the abdominal muscles and so on.

You are now set; go!

- Begin by letting your head that now sits on a relaxed neck move from side to side. That way, you are helping release the tension that may be in your neck muscles. Once you do that, you will feel your body generally relaxing.

- It is now time to address your mind. Sweep out all thoughts from your mind. Oh – and how is that possible? You may try to forget the issue of your college fees but then the thought of the energy bills surfaces. And when you have just managed to ignore that one the image of that colleague who sabotages your work in the office jumps in. Looks like this is the real sabotage against opening your third eye – lots to worry about in life!

But gladly, there is a trick. Do you hear that humming of your old fridge that seems destined to go on for eternity? You can choose to focus on it single mindedly. Alternatively, you can focus on your breathing rhythm – in, out, in, out... Whatever you focus on let your mind not be distracted from it.

Alright! But a tough call it is. No – do not fret about attaining perfection. Rome was not built in a day and you do not expect to master this technique overnight. So, cut yourself some slack. If a thought lands from nowhere – well, you know it is from some corner of your mind – just acknowledge it has had the better of you and switch your focus back to the one thing you chose for concentration.

How long do you remain in the state of meditation?

Well, you need to aim at 30 minutes in the least. However, you do not have to stick to the minimum because you know what? You often find yourself wasting the initial 10 to 15 minutes of your session, trying to get rid of all the junk that has accumulated in your mind from the daily hustles. In fact, you can refer to those first many minutes as your transition period from the normal chaotic world to your peaceful meditative state.

How often should I meditate?

Hey! You cannot have enough of a good thing. But since the reality of life is such that you cannot meditate as often as monks do, spare some time every day just for that. Once you make daily meditation part of you, you will begin to notice some elevated level of consciousness.

And when you are seriously pressed for time?

Well, just know the secret of what you want and make it happen. Even five minutes or less will do. Yes – you can do it. Once you have mastered the art of meditation, you can just leave the scene where everyone else is, dash to the toilet – supposedly, and not for real – and just go to a secluded place and have a couple of minutes' session of meditation. You will join the rest of your pack feeling more relaxed and with more heightened level of comprehension.

Some simple but important things to note:

- If you keep thinking about how much time is remaining for your meditation session to end, it means you will be distracted very often. Why not solve this problem by setting a timer? So, yours is to concentrate with no excuse to stray. After all, once your session is up, your timer will ring.

- You can meditate even as you go about some chores. Just like you can send a prayer to the Divine even when you are not in a place of worship, so too can you put your mind into meditating mode anytime, anywhere. For instance, when you are busy brushing your teeth, something that we know is very repetitive and routine; you can deliberately focus on the movement of your brush while keeping all other thoughts out. You will effectively manage to handle two things in one move – you will have clean teeth and a clear, focused mind.

Here is another angle to opening your third eye:

The inadvertent way.

The way your third eye opens up in under this banner is surely inadvertent. You do not go out to open it and you do not strategize about it. Yet it happens. Here are some ways you can abruptly find yourself with a radically high level of intuition in a way you never experienced before:

After experiencing a near death situation

Instances have been known where ordinary people like you became psychics after surviving near fatal accidents. You have the mediums John Holland and Maureen Hancock of the US as great examples whose heightened psychic abilities developed after serious accidents.

After losing someone you love

Inevitably, even people who are ordinarily not spiritual become spiritual in the course of grieving for someone they loved. And as they let themselves get spiritual comfort, they get their third eye opened even though that was not a planned move.

After giving birth to a child

Automatically, your senses are on high alert when you have a newborn. You want to protect the vulnerable baby and ensure it is comfortable at all times. That in itself is a way of opening your third eye as your intuition heightens.

Undertaking energetic healing

If you have sessions of energetic healing, say hypnosis or something like *Reiki*, which is a form of physical therapy, you can have your third eye opening. Such sessions activate your sixth sense and raise the frequency of your vibrations.

Just so you know, those extraordinary ways of activating your third eye are not exhaustive. If you look at the thread that cuts across all of them, you can safely come to the conclusion that any life shaking event can cause an alert in your system and hence a heightened level of intuition – activating your third eye.

Chapter 5:
Applying the Trataka Technique of Meditation

You can open your third eye by following the technique popularly known as trataka. Trataka simply means gazing in common parlance. And the gazing in this meditation technique refers to the kind of concentration that you do, focusing on one particular point for a prolonged period of time.

Exactly How Does Trataka Open The Third Eye?

First of all, you need to know that this technique is based on the spiritual belief system that holds the contention that the third eye is right where your sixth chakra is: right on your forehead, between your eyebrows. And you also need to appreciate the importance of the sixth chakra so that you can appreciate its relevance here. If you have no idea, just understand that chakras are points in your body where spiritual energy converges to bring harmony to your overall being; and different chakras have different roles.

When the energy is flowing nicely within the sixth chakra, you find yourself aware of your surroundings, in a way that you can sense danger if it is lurking somewhere, and you can get encouraged if there is positive energy around you. So it is just as well that when you use the trataka technique, the spot you focus on is right on your brow where that sixth chakra is. And once you manage to do that successfully, then you will be increasing your sense of awareness – what you perceive without seeing with your two naked eyes. And you will have succeeded in opening your third eye.

Here Are The Steps Of Trataka:

- Sit upright on the floor.

- Ensure your spine is particularly upright.

- You need to position your legs in a cross-legged manner.

In this technique too, if you cannot sit on the floor, it is fine for you to sit comfortably but upright in a chair.

- Now shut your two eyes.

- With your eyes well closed, do breath in and out three consecutive times.

- Still with your eyes closed, try and focus on your forehead; the place you recall we traced the 6th chakra. When talking on focusing, you practically try to draw your eyes towards that middle part of your brow.

- As you do so, begin to count the numbers from 100, one by one backwards up to 1. Just leave about two seconds between one digit and the next. In short, while sitting in an upright position and with your body well relaxed, and also with your eyes closed and focused on your brow, you begin to count silently in your mind: 100, 99, 98, 97, 96, 95, ...1.

In the meantime, do not be surprised to feel some strain on your eyes. You can be sure it does not graduate to pain or anything unpleasant. It is a kind of strain that you soon get accustomed to and actually enjoy it.

What else transpires?

- There is also some sensational feeling around your point of focus; indicating that something is happening to your third eye.

- Keep your focus steady, still on the middle of your brow.

- Your third eye continues to open and soon you begin to see thoughts; seeing things like the way you see things in a dream.

- Keep your focus still on the position of the third eye until you have successfully done 10 to 15 minutes.

- Great! Now you can allow yourself to reverse your focus to your surroundings, but still with your eyes closed.

- Let your eyes relax.

- Let your focus now leave your third eye and return to normalcy.

- Remain still for a couple of minutes.

- With your eyes relaxed, draw air in and out three times; inhaling and exhaling.

- Now you can open your two eyes slowly.

- Great! You are done with your Trataka Meditation.

And, without a doubt, you have succeeded in doing two things:

- You have exercised your physical eyes in a way that leaves them healthier.

- You have learnt how to concentrate and draw the power of intuition.

Care that you need to take:

It is normal to feel some warmth around the area of your third eye as you meditate. But if that warmth graduates to intense warmth or even heat, that is a sign that your intensity is opening an even deeper spiritual path. In fact, sometimes that effect manifests in form of irritation. And since that reaction is in the realm of things you need to rehearse for prior to this experience, it is best that you interrupt your trataka meditation forthwith.

Chapter 6:
Using Yoga to Enhance the Power of Your 3rd Eye

Do you need the working of your third eye being consistently optimal or fluctuating at will? Of course whatever makes you enlightened, relaxed and happy had better remain working well at all times. Unfortunately, there are lots of things that happen around you that are a threat to the good working of your third eye. You may possibly be aware, for instance, that negative thinking can blur your vision from the perspective of your third eye. Being fearful is another factor. And there are lots more of those apparently trivial things that can turn you to an ordinary Joe who does not see beyond the physical things that are within view of ordinary sight.

Fortunately, there are other helpful ways beyond what has already been mentioned in this book that can have your sixth chakra well balanced. Yes, well balanced, because it is when your 6th chakra is well aligned and facilitating great flow of energy that you feel great, intuitive and free. And that is how you get to know things beyond the ordinary folk whose 3rd eye is just but a little crack on the pineal gland.

How Yoga enhances the working of your 3rd Eye

Any idea what yoga is? Well, different people may have different ways of explaining it, but the long and short of it is that it is a kind of science whose practice began ages ago, which gets you into a tranquil state where you know no turbulence of thought nor any physical restlessness. At that moment, it is like everything is still. You are just in a quiet and serene state. You are not thinking about the future, analyzing your past or even worrying about the present – you just are.

Now what is the essence of just being? Good question – it is in just being that you get to the heightened level of self awareness. And in this state, you are one happy human being. Ever heard of that verse in the Christian Holy Book, the Bible, which says be still and you will know that I'm God? Well, that is a spiritual angle to stillness and quietude. And you know the level of awareness you are looking to achieve by opening your third eye is one that is spiritual. It is that awareness that adds great meaning to your life so that you are no longer afraid of the brevity of your physical life.

So in yoga, what you do is stop focusing on outward influences to direct your thinking. Instead, you direct your energy inwards to your mind, where you let that intense energy enhance your consciousness.

Again, why is it important that your third eye is open? Simple:

- You want to see beyond the physical

- You want better perception of things and situations

- You want to have high intuition

- You would like to enjoy great dreams

- You would like to have great visions

- You want to have great imagination

- You want to be highly inspired

- You want that guidance that comes from within you

- You want to be able to link the physical and spiritual worlds in a harmonious way.

- You want to visualize your existence in totality – every aspect of your life being an integral part of your life as a whole.

It will help you to know that in the case of opening or enhancing your third eye, some yoga poses are most preferable.

Thunderbolt pose – Vajrasana

The term's first part, *Vajra*, bears the meaning of thunderbolt, while the second part, *asana*, is a particular posture that you sit in while performing some form of yoga – actually the *hatha* yoga. Vajra is actually god's own weapon – god Indra, who is heaven's ruler.

In this thunderbolt post, you get your body purified, in preparation for meditation. And generally when doing *hatha* yoga, you develop a good level of awareness and also control over your body's internal state.

How does the thunderbolt pose help?

Plenty:

- It tones down your personal criticism; that inner critic that causes you to judge yourself harshly leading you to feel terrible about yourself.

- It creates a great observer of you

What this essentially means is that you are able to look at your thoughts without being emotionally affected by them. So it is not like someone is asking you to assume you have no thoughts – no. But how you handle those thoughts is what is important to the working of your third eye. So you are observing your thoughts with strictly no engagement with them.

Still, make no mistake about this state of observation. Although those thoughts do not influence you, the impact you have on them from sheer observation is significant. Of course you will be observing them with your intense energy, and so inevitably, you are going to impact them; and that is in a good way. That is the reason the outcome of this thunderbolt pose is you feeling whole again.

How to form the thunderbolt pose:

- Sit down. How?

    o Well – you sit on your own heels and with your knees apart

    o In the meantime, you have your spine straight

Feeling a bit uncomfortable, particularly your knees? No problem – a towel beneath your butt will do

- Handle your palms well. How?

    o By placing them right on your thighs

- Try not to strain your spine. How?

    o By releasing your entire weight downwards through your seat bones

- Now inhale deep through your nose and then exhale in a similar fashion

- Allow your spine to have a feel of its full length upwards

- Release your shoulders so that they feel no tension

- At the same time, let your shoulders spread wide

- Adjust your gaze. How? Easy:

  o In front of you. How far? Say, about a stretch of 1.2 meters

  o And mind your focus – should be on the floor; or down on the ground

- In your pose, let your deep inhaling and exhaling continue

- And continue to observe your thoughts.

In your quietude and pose, you will notice your thoughts moving along like clouds passing through a sky lit by the glow of a sunny day. The important thing for you is to remember – just observing; no engaging, as far as those thoughts are concerned.

Can you now see what you will effectively be doing? You will be relaxing your body as well as your mind as you play the detached observer.

And what are the benefits of this form of yoga?

- You will find yourself being more compassionate with yourself

- You will be able to identify behavior patterns that are not helpful to you

- You will be in a position to design the changes necessary for those awful behavior patterns for your own good

- You will feel in harmony with other people in your life and with those around you

- You will practically experience relatively much more peace than before

- You will feel even more knowledgeable deep within you

- You will experience increased joy

Downward Facing Dog – Adho Mukha Svanasana

This is one pose that prepares you for a headstand. A headstand is bound to increase the flow of blood into your head, and so this pose is meant to help you handle that. In this Downward Facing Dog pose, ensure your focus is on your third eye.

- This is how you form the pose:

- Use the floor where you are standing on for kneeling.

- Spread a mat on the floor on which you will have a grip as you do your yoga pose

- While in a kneeling position, go on your fours with your back straight out; that is, flat.

- Stretch your good hands forwards a little more, and let your fingers spread out. In fact, not just the fingers – even your palms need to be spread out flat. Generally your hands should be firm on the ground.

- Now the moves:

  o Prepare to exhale. As you exhale, straighten out your legs

  o And your feet need to be steady and flat on the floor even at that time

  o In the meantime, your tailbone is being lifted upwards

  o You also need to keep lifting your seat bones to the direction of the ceiling

  o And your tailbone, meanwhile, is kind of pulling away from your pelvis

- Make your knees feel strong ensuring they do not get locked

- Essentially, in the Adho Mukha Svanasana pose, your arms are straightened out; your hands open and spread out on the mat; with your palms well pressed on the mat.

How long is the recommended time to remain in this Downward Facing Dog yoga pose?

Well, one to three minutes make the ideal duration.

And how precisely do you benefit?

- Your mind calms down

- Your entire body gets energized

Chapter 7:
Using Essential Oils to Enhance the Clarity of Your 3rd Eye

What are essential oils anyway? Well, these are oils that are natural and which are derived from plants, seeds or other natural sources basically by means of distillation. And that is not all. These oils bear the fragrance of their mother source. You can now see why it is easy for essential oils to be of help when it comes to enhancing the power of your third eye – they have significant natural energy that gets your sixth chakra in a desirable balance.

Essential oils actually have energy frequencies as well as healing properties that are equivalent to those of their natural sources like plants. It is those frequencies and the oils' properties that work within the different levels of being.

Again, what are the significant benefits of essential oils to the third eye?

You get to observe your thoughts with great clarity

You get to see and perceive things better

Your insight on a spiritual level is enhanced

Looking at those benefits just mentioned, do you notice that your third eye does help you with both the sight related to the outside or physical world as well as that which relates to the inner world that is not physical? Physically you see things for what they are without hastening to misjudge them, and spiritually you get to decipher your thoughts with objectivity and wisdom. And, of course, you get to see what many other people may not see – things happening on the higher planes of existence.

Important Points to Note about Your 3rd Eye:

- When you consider your physical make-up, you will find your third eye being associated with your normal eyes, somehow by extension of seeing and perceiving; your pituitary gland; your brain; and also your pineal gland.

- Then come your emotional level, you find your emotional imbalances manifesting in form of:

  o Behavior that indicates denial

  o A tendency to be delusional

  o Suffering nightmares

  o Being engulfed by unjustified fear

- From a mental level perspective, any imbalances on the working of your third eye causes you:

  o To suffer poor memory

  o Become poor at decision making

  o Become slow in comprehending things at an abstract level

  o Find it difficult to appreciate messages conveyed in symbolic language

- At your spiritual level, any imbalances in the workings of your third eye are likely to occasion:

- The condition of being spaced out

- Inability to acknowledge the truth in its depth

- Inability to appreciate connections in issues particularly those that require solving

- The tendency to mistrust your own intuition so that you keep ignoring that persistent inner voice to your own detriment

Popular Essential Oils for the Third Eye

Bay Laurel

How would you describe this essential oil? Obviously, it comes from a plant which has great aroma; one that even produces food seasoning – bay leaf seasoning, actually. It is not surprising, therefore, that the oil itself is aromatic in a spicy way.

Why this sweet aromatic essential oil is great for your third eye:

- It elevates your awareness

- It opens up your perception

- It heightens your level of clairsentience

- It heightens your level of clairvoyance

- It heightens your level of clairaudience

Is the Bay Laurel essential oil a recent discovery as far as raising self awareness and enhancing perception is concerned?

Really, Bay Laurel has been in use for ages in this same regard. In the Greece of old, for instance, people used it to enhance their ability to commune with the Divine. They also used it to be able to comprehend matters of prophetic nature.

Today, the Bay Laurel essential oil works by stimulating your brain such that the ability of your left side of the brain to connect with your right is enhanced. And here we are talking about your rational mind being able to connect with your creative mind respectively. When you are able to synchronize your rational thinking with your creative thinking, it is a sign that your awareness has been awakened. It also means that you are now able to perceive things more holistically.

Jasmine

Like many other essential oils, jasmine is extracted from natural plant – this one being the shrub, *Jasminum grandiflorum*. And it is the same one you may hear referred to as *Royal Jasmine*. And some people still call it *Jati*. Other times you may hear this essential oil producing species being referred to as *Catalonian* or even *Spanish Jasmine*.

Whatever name it goes by, the essential oil extracted from this plant is sweet and rich in floral smell. And this plant that is a climbing shrub with an exotic look produces the oil through the method of steam distillation.

How does Jasmine help enhance your third eye?

First of all, it is important to appreciate the importance with which Jasmine has been held from time immemorial. In India, just for example, this essential oil has been:

- Associated with the moon

- In magic related rituals

- In rituals of healing

And today, for the sake of enhancing the abilities of your third eye, you use the Jasmine essential oil:

- To uplift your mood and have a positive outlook to things

- To help you get in touch with your soul at a very deep level

- To help you get in touch with deeply buried emotions of pain

- To enhance your powers of intuition

- To stimulate your overall senses in a powerful way

- To enable you to get connected with the wholeness of the universe

Palo Santo

This essential oil gets extracted from a wild tree found mainly in Mexico, Venezuela and other countries within South America. This tree is traditionally considered mystical and so having its product associated with enhancing the power of the third eye is nothing surprising. In fact, the name Palo Santo is Spanish and its meaning is literally *Holy Wood*. And as you may recall, the third eye gets you to travel spiritually to higher realms once it is well open and the sixth chakra is well balanced.

In the days of old, the Palo Santo wood was:

- Burnt to produce essence

- Used as a purifying agent during particular ceremonies

From a desirability point of view, the Palo Santo essence:

- Has a rich aroma

- Has a sweet aroma which you can link with that of the citrus family where the mother plant belongs. In fact, you can detect some lemon like scent; like mint or even pine.

The Palo Santo essence makes great preparation when you are readying yourself for connection to higher realms like the astral plane. And how does it prepare your grounds for this connection?

- Helping you be in shape for meditation

- Heightening your spiritual awareness

- Helping you be in shape for prayer

- Helping you in cleansing yourself

- Enhancing your ability to understand the subtle realms once you have effectively made the connection

Carrot Seed

Where does this oil really come from? Well, this is some high quality oil that you get from the carrot seed. And this seed is from the plant they call *Daucus Carota*. You can detect its naturalness from a mile away – its woody and earthy smell that happens to be sweet too. And it has color shades beginning from amber to something like a pale orange leaning on to brownish.

This quality oil is great for your third eye particularly in bringing reality into your world. There are times that you may be blurred from distinguishing what is real and what is a figment of your imagination, and in such cases it becomes difficult to forge ahead with decision making. You may not even know what action to take in some circumstances. Moreover, you may be overwhelmed with fear or confusion. But with the use of the carrot seed as your chosen essential oil:

- The health of your eyesight is taken care of

In fact, this is not a recent development. Over the years, carrot seed essential oil has been known to heal physical eyesight.

- It is also great for your spiritual awakening

And when the oil makes you spiritually aware, you are able to appreciate reality as it is and as it continues to unfold in your life. This is great in keeping you grounded.

- Carrot seed creates harmony between you in the physical and you in the spiritual arenas

As such it helps you to enjoy experiences within your subtle bodies even as you stay in your physical form. Of course, such experiences are not just a source of knowledge for you but also a way of spiritual enlightenment that continues to enhance your grounding.

- The oil also prepares you for vision

And when you already have visions, this oil makes them more vivid.

On the overall, using the carrot seed essential oil is great for your spiritual insight.

Melissa

Did you know that this oil is taken to be the best in the field of aromatherapy? With the citrus scent and a great freshness and lightness, this oil, which also goes by the reference lemon balm, is considered a great anti-depressant. It is a type of oil derived from a natural plant named Melissa officinalis, found around the Mediterranean and places such as Europe towards the south-central region.

In working with your third eye, the Melissa essential oil:

- Helps to open your heart chakra

- Is also great in stimulating your pineal gland

- As a consequence, helps you to appreciate realities that are not necessarily commonplace, and which you normally would not understand.

- Makes you better placed to access vibrations that are much higher than yours

This is a great way for you to connect with higher realms, your higher worlds of existence from where you derive spiritual understanding, calmness and hope.

Chamomile

You may see this one sometimes being spelt as camomile. It is an essential oil that is derived from the family of plants looking like daisies, but is called *Asteraceae*. People generally know it for its calming effect and its ability to alleviate anxiety.

How, then, does chamomile help your third eye in its function?

Mainly, your chamomile essential oil targets your nervous system

Obviously, when you are suffering anxieties and different fears, and when you are fidgety about some uncertainties, it is your nervous system that is adversely affected first and foremost – the reason we describe it as having nerves. Needless to say, this condition can hurt your energy flow and particularly the kind of flow needed for the optimal working of your third eye. So, your chamomile works towards:

- Calming your edgy nerves

- Soothing your whole system

- Helping you realize the impulses being triggered by your ego

- Helping you to see and acknowledge the influence your ego is having on you

- After seeing and acknowledging the patterns that are a product of your ego, you get to understand that those patterns do not necessarily define you. And so Chamomile opens up your third eye in a way that leads you to appreciate that you are higher than what you manifest physically and emotionally.

- Bringing out the reality that your projections do not define you

In summary, what chamomile does is to take your understanding to a much higher level and you begin to observe your ego driven behaviour from an objective perspective – like an observing witness. This experience contributes immensely to the opening of your third eye and keeping it balanced.

Rose

Whatever the rose essence is? It is that essence extracted from a shrub or some sort of prickly bush that originated within the temperate regions of the world. However, the family of roses is quite wide with species reaching a hundred, and so various kinds can be found beyond the temperate areas too.

And how does the rose essence help your third eye? Well:

- It calms you down

- It makes you relax

- It penetrates your physical body and with its vibrations reaches your subtle bodies, making them all aligned and working in rhythm

- It creates a good balance in your energy flow

- It brings harmony into you as a whole

- It stimulates your mind, something that is helpful when it comes to awareness of the self and that of your surrounding

- It elevates your mind and that has the impact of heightening your intuition

- On the overall, the rose essence gives you a sense of wellbeing.

Clary Sage

This essential oil is extracted from a herb that goes by the same name. Sometimes, too, it is simply known as Clary; or passes as Salvia sclarea. The herb is most common in areas to the north of the Mediterranean. You will also easily find it in regions on the north of Africa and parts of Central Asia. This aromatic herb belongs to the mint family and so you can imagine its lovely scent.

Traditionally, this herb has not been known just for its culinary use, but also for its natural healing properties, including the power to alleviate eye problems. So, it is not surprising that today its essential oil is associated with the healthy working of your third eye.

When it comes to the operation of your third eye, how energy flows through your other chakras and the rest of your body has an inevitable impact. Similarly, when your third eye is open and working well, the rest of your body works relatively well. That is why the Clary Sage essential oil comes in handy when:

- It heals you of headaches and even migraines

- It works towards reversing autism

- It works towards healing epilepsy

- It works towards alleviating seizures

On the overall, the Clary is helpful in reducing or even alleviating any semblance of seizure activity in your brain. This leaves your brain calm and stable, a state that brings the tranquillity needed for higher exploration and intuition.

Chapter 8:
Using Crystals to Balance Your 3rd Eye Chakra

*Is it no*t obvious by now that for you to function well you need the chakra of your third eye well balanced? Yet as you know, what you wish for does not always match the reality of life. That is one reason you need interventions along the way. In your case here, sometimes you get the energies of the brow chakra either vibrating on an overdrive or other times they are much lower than optimal. This impacts your physical as well as mental state and you can be sure it is not for the better.

What are some of the physical functions that usually go wrong when your brow chakra is not working well?

As you may recall, your brow chakra is the one associated with your third eye; the reason you find some cultures putting a mark on the spot between their eyebrows just above the nose. And like all the other major chakras that you have, the brow chakra has physical areas of the body that it influences. Those are the ones that are adversely affected when your brow chakra has some kind of block. In summary, when the energies and vibrations from your brow chakra are not doing well:

- The normal functions of your pituitary gland are adversely affected

- In actual fact, the functions of your endocrine system as a whole are negatively affected

- The balancing of the functions of your left and right hemispheres of your brain is negatively affected

- Your immune system tends to get compromised

- The synapses of your brain are affected in an adverse manner, which means that the brain's natural impulses are not going to move as they should. And as you can imagine that in itself can adversely affect other functions of your body with poor co-ordination and all.

Physical features directly affected by the state of your brow chakra, and by extension your third eye, include:

- Your eyes

- Your ears

- Your sinuses

- Your face in general

What are some of the metaphysical functions that usually go wrong when your brow chakra is not working well?

Of course, you appreciate that your third eye is responsible for more than just your physical welfare, unlike, most of your other chakras. So when it is not in good balance, even your abstract thinking; your attitude; your perception and intuition; all these and more of a subtle nature are bound to be adversely affected. Generally, the metaphysical functions you can be certain would be affected include:

- Your sub-conscious mind

- Your level of clairvoyance

- Your level of creative imagination

- Your ability to visualize things

- The way you intuitively perceive things

And you know when you think of intuition you need not confine yourself to only the aspect of sensing things by impulse – no. Intuition has that basic element of leading you to appreciating the truth about things; that is, facing the way things are without necessarily engaging in logical thinking, reasoning or even justification.

How does your attitude affect your third eye?

The fact that the attitude you bear affects how your third eye works is easy to appreciate. This is because, as already mentioned, your third eye influences your body as a whole, including your ability to visualize things beyond their physical status. If your attitude is positive, you are able to visualize possibilities of success in your life, while if your attitude is negative, you tend to be pessimistic about your life. Whatever you visualize then instigates your actions and you can end up being motivated to improve your life or have your spirit dampened in a way that leads to apathy.

Also in reality, even as your attitude influences the way you act, it can also be a sign of the state of your mind. In short, it is easy to tell when a person's third eye is not in good shape by the attitude they manifest.

Here are attitudes associated with a brow chakra that is over-active:

- You become a worrier – always worrying about things even those that do not heavily impact your life

- You tend to be fearful – having the tendency to see things and situations as threatening, and even fearing possibilities and not realities

- The tendency to be overly sensitive

In such times, people around you tend to walk on eggshells for fear of offending you. Sometimes this attitude may manifest in you being defensive or even too critical of others.

- Displaying tendencies of being impatient

- Tending to belittle other people's behavior

- Getting spaced out

Here are attitudes associated with a brow chakra that is under-active:

- You become a doubting person; including harboring lots of self-doubt

- You tend to become jealous of the talents of other people

- You become very forgetful

- You tend to be strongly superstitious

- You become unjustifiably fearful

- You tend to worry too much

Clearly, you are not in a good place when your third eye is agape with your brow chakra on an overdrive, and neither are you in a good place when your third eye is just but a mere crack with an underactive brow chakra.

Luckily, there are some natural crystals that are accessible all over the world which you can use to awaken your third eye where it is working below par, and to tone down the energy of your third eye where it is working excessively. As you will see in later chapters, each crystal has its aura color and each aura color has its specific vibrations and energy frequencies. Those are aspects that determine what crystal is fitting for what chakra and in what circumstances.

Here are the ideal crystal colors to wear or carry close to you when your brow chakra is overworking:

- Orange and close shades of it

- Gold

- Green and its associated shades

In case you wish to use additional crystals at the time of meditation to enhance the power of balancing your brow chakra from an overdrive, the best crystals to use and in small doses happen to be:

- Those that are clear

- Those ones of a purple color

- Crystals that are dark blue

- Those ones that are indigo

Incidentally, these are the same colors that are recommended for use when you are saying affirmations.

Here are the ideal crystal colors to wear or carry close to you when your brow chakra is underactive:

- Purple colored crystals

- Crystals that are dark blue

- Crystals bearing the indigo color

Do you know what crystals are best when you are saying various affirmations?

First of all, you need to underline the fact that there are crystal colors that are great in invoking your intuition. They heighten your awareness as the power of your third eye continues to develop. Those are the crystals you go for when you want to balance your brow chakra and improve the working of your third eye. Those crystals include the indigo; the blue; and the purple ones.

And you know what else those crystals do?

Well, they help you in your personal development as well as personal growth

Exactly how do you use the crystals for self development as well as growth?

Easy – you learn the positive affirmations that are suitable for your purpose, and then choose to have specific crystals with you while saying those affirmations. This will help you make your life better by:

- Enabling you to understand yourself better

- Helping you to understand your friends better

- Helping you to understand individual members of your family better

- Helping you to understand your co-workers better

Naturally, by understanding yourself and others, you get to appreciate yourself and the rest of the people whom you interact with. In the process, you get to appreciate your strengths along with your weaknesses and you also do the same as far as the other people are concerned. It is the surest way of living in peace with yourself and in harmony with others. And you can thus use your areas of strength to make yourself better, deal aptly with your weaknesses and also tap into the strengths of others to complement what you have.

Here are helpful crystals and explanations to the affirmations that best go with them:

Purple agate

Did you know that this crystal that belongs to the Chalcedony family is known for its power in meditation as well as spiritual transformation? No wonder it comes in handy when you are saying your affirmations particularly those related to your third eye. As you hold or wear your purple agate, affirm that you are actually grounded in your spirituality. State that spirituality is integrated into your daily life. Assert that you are intuitive and also insightful.

Amethyst

Did you know that the amethyst crystal has over the years been associated with protecting its wearer from drunkenness? While this might be sound interesting, you need to have in mind the fact that a drunken mind cannot comprehend and appreciate things as well as a sober mind. And in matters of intuition and high level awareness, which is what the third eye is about, you need soberness. And, of course, what follows is sobriety as you evaluate issues of this world as well as those of higher planes.

With the amethyst in your possession, assert that you see, you sense and you also know that your life is actually magical. Emphasize that you usually have pleasant dreams. Declare that you release every habit that no longer works for your highest good. Say that you have a strong connection with your spiritual guides as well as your angels. Also declare that you are intensely clairvoyant.

Clear Aprophyllite

Did you know that the pyramid crystal is not just clear but also extremely bright and reflective of light? You can equate that brightness and clearness to the crystal's clarity regarding matters pertaining to the third eye. This one is among the most suitable crystals to help you reach your higher realms; the one to bring you wisdom through your subconscious.

While in the possession of this crystal, declare that you have a great connection with the Divine and that your meditation session is literally easy as well as natural. Affirm that you have enjoyed great experiences in meditation. Assert that you are highly intuitive. Declare that you are one to get things done and that you usually accomplish whatever it is that needs accomplishing. State categorically that you have mental clarity.

Clear Quartz

Did you know that for all its clearness this six sided prism that is Clear Quartz holds the whole color spectrum within it? And from time immemorial, different cultures have linked it to the Divine.

Declare, while in possession of this crystal, that there is a greater perspective from which you see life. State your belief that your intuitive skills are continually on the increase. Declare how greatly intuitive you are and also assert that what you adhere to in life is your internal guidance system.

Blue Goldstone

Are you aware that this crystal is referred to as the master healer? And it is mainly because it is great at connecting you with the Divine where no problem is too big to be solved.

With this crystal in your possession, declare how extremely clairvoyant you are. Say that you always receive messages from your guides as well as angels. Say also how grateful you are for that inner guidance that you have and declare that you have trust in it.

Lapis Lazuri

Remember this crystal is a metaphoric rock that has a bright blue color. While wearing or carrying it, declare categorically that the great wisdom of past cultures is properly stored in your very own cells, bones as well as muscles, and that it is accessible to you whenever you need it. State your belief that your third eye is open sufficiently for you at this particular stage in life. Assert how greatly intuitive you are and how consistently you keep receiving messages as well as guidance. Plainly say that you are calm and also relaxed.

Selenite

As you hold close this transparent crystal, state clearly that you are firmly linked to the Divine. State too that your intuitive skills keep improving on a daily basis. Declare that the guidance you follow is the one directly from your guides and your angels. Affirm that you have a physical structure that is strong and also well aligned.

Sodalite

This crystal happens to be blue and comes from an alkaline rock. The affirmation you need to say when in possession of this crystal is one that asserts your position that you bear calm emotions. Affirm that not only is your mind clear but it is also relaxed. Say that you are intuitive. Declare that whatever inflammation your body may bear, or even your mind or your spirit, is in good balance and is for your utmost good.

Falcon's Eye

When in possession of this bluish crystal that is hailed for its help in astral travel, declare that you are capable of visualizing your reality into actual being. Declare how insightful you are and that you happen to have extraordinary moments of great inspiration. State clearly that you are in the habit of receiving and also interpreting messages coming from up the heavenly realm. Affirm that you can see life's bigger picture and are capable of acting accordingly. State your assurance that you are grounded and also protected in your spiritual development.

Chapter 9:
Meditation and Thinking are not synonymous

Have you realized there is a great possibility of thinking yourself to depression? Jokes aside, there are people who have thought their way into the sanatorium and I bet they knew nothing about meditation. Yet, some people think when you talk of meditation you mean pondering over things. Which things? That is important. If you are turning your problems over in your head, analyzing them and thinking about how badly you are because of the situation you are in, that is sheer thinking – not meditating.

But does meditation not deal with the mind?

Oh sure! Meditation does deal with the mind just like thinking. But then again, unlike in thinking, it does not:

- Embrace negative thinking

- Encourage you to beat yourself up

- Involve analyzing your daily plans and trying to shuffle them in your priority list

- Tire your mind

- Give you either physical or even emotional stress

So what does meditation do that is not part of thinking?

In meditation, you:

- Essentially clear your mind of all thoughts

- You let your entire mind succumb to relaxation without any list of things to do

- You allow your body to relax and rid itself of any physical tension

- Connect with your spiritual self

- You release all sense of urgency that may try to set in

How does meditation help you as opposed to thinking?

- You breath clearly without any impediment

- Your mind is at ease

- You are able to focus inwards

- Your mind is fully awakened and you become self aware

- You are free from worldly distractions

- Your chest opens up in a pleasant way

- Your body relaxes

- You have full control of your mind

- Your entire self is calm and at peace

With all the goodness, why is meditation not common to everyone?

The reality is that children are taught from an early age to identify things in their surroundings; appreciate the colors that they see; learn how to identify other people's actions; and generally practice how to deal with things physical. And so when stress sets in, you take it as part and parcel of life; something you have no choice but to live with.

When then do you listen to your inner feelings? And when do you learn how to reach high levels of intuition? When, if ever, do you get in touch with your spiritual side? When ever do you learn how to be at peace with yourself and closing all else worldly away? When do you practice the art of being in harmony with nature? Never – until you learn the art of meditation and realize that stress is avoidable. With meditation, you learn that you have ability to understand even that which you cannot see with your physical eyes. And with that life becomes more meaningful and more fulfilling.

How to avoid the toxicity of thinking and embrace the benefits of meditation

This is not in any measure rocket science. With practice, you will manage to identify unhelpful thoughts and refuse to give them attention.

- Avoid being stuck in stereotypes and presumptions

- Open up to creativity and possibilities driven from your inner self

- Discard beliefs that are self limiting

- Ignore any thoughts that limit your potential

In short, you can control and direct your thought stream. Think of your mind as a radio capable of voicing ideas from different stations. Do you not change the station when it is not helpful to you or when it is uninteresting? In fact, do you not change the station fast when you realize what it is giving you is sheer propaganda geared towards twisting your thinking and jeopardizing your well being? Right – do the same with the wiring in your mind. Direct your thinking towards the thoughts that promote your well being and your relationship between you and other people; and between you and the universe at large.

Chapter 10:
Using Open Portal Technique to Open the 3rd Eye

This technique that is referred to as Open Portal has a slightly different style. The results are, however, not affected in any way. You still get your third eye open and you feel a great sense of awareness and cognition.

This is how you implement this technique:

- You lie down flat out on the ground or such other surface.

- While in that relaxed position, lift one index finger and touch the area right between your eyebrows. That is the point just above your nose bridge.

- Use that forefinger to press that spot in between your eyebrows, moving it in circular movements and in a clockwise direction. This is effectively some form of massage.

- Do the massage for something like 30 seconds and then remove your finger.

- Very likely, you will be left feeling some swirling sensation on that spot you just rubbed, even with your index finger already released. That is actually eergy moving within you.

- Now move your eyeballs in an upwards direction. That movement of the eyeballs should be something like 20°.

- With this eye movement, you will, very likely, experience a swirling feeling that is even stronger than before.

- Now pull in air through your nose – inhaling.

- At this juncture, you will feel some energy movement right from your feet. The route that energy takes is from the soles; through the calves; via your legs; through your groin; passing through your hips and your torso; upwards via your spine; right through your throat; entering your head to reach the spot where energy has been swirling.

- As you now exhale, you will feel some pulsation and strength in that area of your third eye; and you will experience some powerful glow.

- Do a fresh round of inhalation and feel the energy traveling within you right from the soles of your feet; upwards through your lower and to your upper body; the same way the energy traveled in the first round. On exhalation, the energy you feel at that spot in between your eyebrows is even more intense.

- Now that you have mastered this art of inhalation and exhalation; and focusing on the movement of your energy from your feet up to your brow, you need to repeat that exercise until you hit 33 times – considering both inhalations and exhalations.

- After successfully doing this exercise, you will have opened your third eye. You will even be feeling the swirling effect even without touching your forehead.

- Within no time, you will be able to summon the swirling effect without having to touch your forehead or even doing any of those exercises.

- To keep the power of your third eye going, and even to make it even stronger, it is advisable that you do that routine of massaging your forehead and monitoring the movement of energy from your feet up to your forehead every time before you get up in the morning.

- Do the routine before you go to bed too every night.

That is a way of keeping your intuitive power up – keeping your third eye open.

To enhance your understanding of how this open portal technique works, you just need to imagine an indigo rose flower with its attractive petals well rounded to form the open flower. The swirling effect you feel in the middle of your forehead corresponds to the energy that swirls through the unfolding rose. You need to realize that the 6th chakra is symbolized by the indigo color.

Chapter 11:
2-Tier Technique to Open the 3rd Eye

The 1st Awakening

This stage is primarily about connecting with that seat of the soul – the third eye. Which one, you may ask. This is the pineal gland, that tiny place where the famous philosopher of French descent, Rene Descartes, believed your soul resides. And that place, incidentally, happens to be the fundamental link between your body and your mind.

Question: If truly every person has this very important gland, why are many people unaware of their third eye?

Sincere answer: In all honesty, many people are average in many things. And it takes some prompting or some initiative to excel and leave the realm of the average. And when it comes to appreciating and opening your third eye, this is what this book aims for – to get you from the view of the average person, to the different views of a person with higher, more developed intuition.

So, what we are in effect saying is that for an average person, the pineal gland just performs its biological role of secreting melatonin, that hormone that prepares you for night hours and consequently, sleep. However, with appropriate techniques and practice, you can open your third eye – activate that soul seat – and join the people with enhanced mental and intellectual vision.

The 1st stage

This stage is simple, but it needs to be practiced well. This is how you go about it:

- Sit upright somewhere – on the floor or even on some furniture

- Inhale air, as usual, through the nose, only this time you pull in the air slowly into your lungs

- Hold that inhaled air for the longest time you comfortably can

- When it comes to your mouth, of course, the normal thing would be to have it closed – not this time, though. Even without opening it wide, you need to part your teeth some bit, so that the tip of your tongue pushes through your front teeth a little bit.

- Let your tongue put some pressure against your teeth the way you do when you are preparing to say the sound, 'th', as in the word 'the', as you prepare to exhale.

- Now do the actual exhaling, releasing the air in a slow motion through your teeth. And as you release the long stream of air, you will be producing a sound like 'th - h – h – o – h – h'. In short, your tongue will be making vibrations between the teeth.

What is the impact of this procedure?

- Well, for one, you will feel the air exiting through the place of contact between tongue and teeth.

- Your jaw and also your cheeks will experience some kind of sensation. That experience may manifest like some sort of pressure.

- You will have a tone vibrate within your third eye.

You may not have the hang of it at first, but with practice you are going to register the expected experience.

- In fact, just after completing those steps of inhaling and exhaling, restart all over, and keep repeating the procedure until you have completed five (5) consecutive rounds.

Is this now the juncture at which you say, time for 1st awakening is up? Well, not yet – you have just completed its first stage.

The 2nd stage

The 2nd stage of this 1st awakening is where you make a repeat of the whole process of stage one. Here you have got to repeat the procedure after 24hrs. This 24hr waiting period gives your system time to take in the effects of your earlier processes. After that first repeat you need to do another one – also after another 24hrs. In short, the session for this 2nd stage ends when you have done the whole procedure in three days consecutively.

So now, yes – you are done with the 1st awakening.

What signs mark the end of that session of pineal gland awakening or 3rd eye opening?

- Expect some headache

- If not a headache, expect to feel some pressure right in the middle of your forehead.

- And so you know it is the real thing, the pressure will tend to emanate from some place about an inch into the inside of your forehead.

- At some point, you may feel some tingling or even throbbing within your forehead one early morning, something that comes close to a goose bump. The feeling could even continue into the day.

- Sometimes you may sense – what we could actually call 'hearing' – sounds ringing inside your head. And those sounds come across as crackling sensations or even light popping.

With those physiological happenings, you are sure your third eye is pretty open.

Beware:

That headache we have mentioned here may actually turn out to be serious migraine, and you would be better lying down to relax. So the best advice for you is to practice your third eye opening sessions in the evenings, when you cannot affect your day work or routine. However, not everyone experiences the migraines – only those whose pineal gland is calcified in a big way.

Do you know the psychic effect of opening your 3ʳᵈ eye?

Well, here is what you should expect after successful opening of your 3ʳᵈ eye, courtesy of the 1ˢᵗ awakening:

- You begin to increase your learning pace

- You find yourself enhancing your retention rate of what you learn

- Your creativity is enhanced

- You get to strengthen your psychic endowments

- If you never knew you had psychic gifts you begin to discover them

- You get to appreciate human auras in a strong way

- You find psychic visions opening – clairvoyance

- You find psychic hearing opening – clairaudience

- You get psychic feeling or touching opening – clairsentience

Let us summarize this section by saying that whereas some level of discomfort is inevitable at this initial stage of activating your pineal gland, the benefits make the whole experience worthwhile. Gladly, many are the people whose only discomfort is the slight pressure on the forehead.

The 2nd Awakening

The presumption here is that you have already gone through the 1st awakening. It is like talking about polishing your draft – of an assignment or anything else for that matter. You cannot have anything to polish, really, unless you have done some groundwork; laid some foundation. And that is what the first awakening was all about – laying foundation for your energy flow. It was precisely about getting your inner energy, that spiritual energy, flowing. And that you have accomplished.

Now for that flow of energy to take on the best rhythm, your body needs a break of somewhere between ten (10) to fourteen (14) days from the time you complete the session for the 1st awakening. Only then can you begin your 2nd awakening session.

Let us begin by whetting your appetite, for here you are talking about a 2nd session of very pleasurable experience – actually qualifying to be called euphoric. It is recommended that you undertake this session once a week – that is enough for this blissful experience.

Here are the steps you undertake:

- While well sat and relaxed, breathe in to your fullest and then hold your breath within as you inwardly count one up to five.

- Then breathe out slowly

- Repeat the process of breathing in and out slowly three more times.

How do you think this will make you feel? I will tell you – well relaxed and actually focused.

From that point henceforth, put your focus on your third eye. With that deliberate focus, believe you me you are going to feel its existence – that pressure that feels within the spot of the third eye. Now undertake the process below:

- Breathe in as deeply as you did during the first awakening.

- Hold onto that breath for the longest you can within comfort, that is, without straining.

- Then release that air through your mouth in slow exhilaration, letting your lips vibrate the word 'May' as the air comes out. In effect, your air should come out with an auto sound of 'M – a – a – a – a – a – a – a – a – y'.

What feeling should you expect at this juncture?

Well, the opening of the third eye is all about energy flow that causes heightened awareness. At this point in time, therefore, you should expect:

- Energy within your head passing through the location of your third eye

- That energy then heading for the middle part of your brain

- Finally that energy landing on the crown chakra, which is at the top part of your head

Mark you all this happens as you exhale air making the 'May' sound. Another important point to note is that you need to be relaxed in all this, because then, you will be able to follow the flow of your energy, effectively focusing on it as it flows through those three stages of third eye, mid-brain and then your head top.

When you are done with that round of inhalation and exhalation, do a repeat four more times. At the end of it all, you will have done five rounds of inhalation and exhalation, focusing on your energy flow, through all the three relevant areas.

How you should expect to feel after this 2nd awakening:

- Soon after the exercises, you are likely to feel a kind of pleasurable lightness

- Sometimes you may feel some tingling in your head

- Other times you could feel some pressure around your crown area

- It is not uncommon to feel a sense of intense euphoria

On the overall, this 2nd awakening gives you some welcome bliss, and the timing of that bliss can vary from one individual to the next. It could come only hours after the third eye awakening process; or even days after.

You know what the icing on the cake is? Well, this blissful state could last for a very long time, almost becoming part of you. As a result, you find yourself enjoying:

- Void meditation

- Clairvoyance

- Enhancement of additional psychic senses

- Enhancement of other paranormal senses

Chapter 12:
Some Facts about Your Pineal Gland

Do you recall the location of your pineal gland? Well, it is right between your northern and southern hemispheres of your head. Oh-oh... And where is that, precisely? Easy – right at the position you can term the centre of your brain.

Now, even when most of the things to do with your third eye are mental and spiritual, it may help somewhat to understand the physical nature and the scientific aspect and workings of your pineal gland. Of course, you may recall the pineal gland passing for the 'seat of the soul' and being able to regulate your sleeping and waking cycle.

In matters physiological, you may wish to know that your pineal gland has a lot to do with:

- Regulating your body temperature

- Controlling your skin color

- Controlling your hair color

- Controlling the color of your eyes

And what you may need to underline about the pineal gland with regard to the powers of the third eye include:

- Being responsible for generating dreams

- Regulating your emotions

- Enhancing your intuition

- Revamping your memory

- Enhancing your learning capacity

All this happens owing to the fact that your pineal gland is directly associated with your 6th chakra, that energy center in between your eye brows; the one they call *ajna*. And once the energy from your sixth chakra works in league with your pineal gland, then you are:

- Able to discern the reality from mere illusion

- Able to evolve and grow spiritually

- In a position to trust your intuition and benefit from it

- Able to enhance your intelligence

Are you eager to know something a little more interesting about the pineal gland?

Well, learned people of old took this tiny organ to be as useless as that piece of muscle in your abdomen – the appendix. Something that creation or the Divine just put there for lack of a better place to place it. But as you have already noted, the pineal cord has very important scientific and spiritual roles to play in your life.

Why not learn a little more about the pineal gland?

It is a tiny piece of muscle, as small as a pea, and it is within your brain's 3rd ventricle

It is named 'pineal' because it has a shape like that of a pine cone; which in Latin is called 'pinea'.

And do not gape in wonder if you hear the pineal gland going by a different name. Some people still refer to it as:

- Pineal Body

- Epiphysis Cerebri

- Conarium

- Eye of Wisdom

- Single Eye

- Eye of Horus

- Ajna Chakra

- The 3rd Eye

It establishes itself properly around the age of puberty

It happens to have its own cornea; its lens; and even its own retina – the same way your physical eyes do

It is the gland credited with producing the 'happy hormone' – serotonin

It is the gland credited too with producing the 'hormone in charge of darkness' – melatonin

It has a role to play in matters of sexual development

It plays an important role in protecting you from free radicals that are, obviously, harmful to your body

It is, however, susceptible to destruction and your apparent addiction to technology does not help matters touching on your pineal gland

At the time you are meditating, your pineal gland is seen to be working side by side with another hormone producing, pea sized gland, the pituitary, which is located at the lower part of your brain. How can you discern that, you may wonder? By the way the two tiny glands are seen vibrating in unison.

The pineal gland is credited with production of dimethyltryptamine, commonly referred to as DMT that substances that is linked with expanding your consciousness.

It receives heavy blood flow only 2nd to the all-important organs; your kidneys

It has the greatest accumulation of fluoride – no wonder it is calcified

It does not respond well to mercury fillings so if you care much about the health of your pineal gland, you may consider an alternative to mercury

You can decalcify the pineal gland somewhat by consuming alkaline water or water that is distilled. And with decalcification, your pineal gland does its functions better.

It is very sensitive to light and is stimulated by it

It is adversely affected by waves of extremely low frequency, otherwise referred to as ELF waves.

During astral projection or when you are trying to enhance lucidity or recalling a dream, it would help the working of your pineal gland if you unplugged every electronic device around you.

Where health is concerned, you can help keep your pineal gland in shape by consuming mugwort; wood betony; alfalfa; parsley; and even gotu kola.

Chapter 13:
The Uniqueness of the Third Eye

In the first chapter, we referred to the third eye as your mind's eye. This is true because it helps you see things that you otherwise would not visualize with your naked eyes. However, it would help you appreciate better the nature of the third eye and how it works if you understood how your spiritual energy navigates within you.

It is not like there exists a compartment in your brain where spiritual energy dwells waiting to be discharged when you want to think deeper and more intuitively. Rather, your spiritual energy is always flowing through your body, ensuring that you have the right emotional balance at any one time. In fact, it is just like the way your blood flows; always in a continuous flow and never halting irrespective of whether you are working or resting. The difference is, however, that blood is physical while spiritual energy is not.

How does spiritual energy flow in your physical body?

Your spiritual energy flows through various energy centers commonly known as chakras. Most traditions take the main chakras to be seven in number although you could have other mini chakras still within your body. When you speak of a chakra, you are essentially referring to an energy field; and so you can appreciate how you can have numerous small energy fields within a system as big as your body.

Now, each of those main energy fields or chakras has great influence on how you feel on the overall, not just physically but also emotionally and spiritually. Again, you need to know that chakras interrelate just as the different organs of your body do. For instance, you know that an aching stomach or inflamed toe will not let you have a good night's sleep even if we tend to associate sleep with the eyes or the brain. Likewise, if your first chakra is blocked and is not facilitating smooth flow of your spiritual energy, it is going to have a negative impact on how you feel on the overall.

That said, each chakra has its role as follows:

First Chakra

This one is found at the base of your spine and is in charge of your physical wellbeing as well as overall feeling of stability. When working well, it makes you fit well within your surrounding and feel grounded in spite of many variables in life. This is the one that actually what goes by the term Root Chakra.

Second Chakra

This chakra that also goes by the reference, Spleen Chakra, is to be found in your abdomen. It is the chakra that enhances your natural sensuality keeping you passionate, creative, and generally confident in your relationships. The term Sacral Chakra also refers to this second chakra.

Third Chakra

This chakra that also goes by the reference, Solar Plexus, lies midway from the navel to the lower part of your sternum. It is known to keep your metabolism going at a healthy rate and your digestion running smoothly. Although this chakra is basically about matters of metabolism, if it gets blocked you become susceptible to different physical ailments including indigestion; high blood pressure; diabetes; fatigue; and a host of other ailments. You even begin to dislike the way you look and you become very sensitive to criticism.

Fourth Chakra

This is the heart chakra, and not surprisingly, it enhances your emotional balance so that you do not harbor jealousies, bitterness and other negative emotions. When working well, it promotes feelings of love and appreciation, and other positive feelings that make you emotionally stable. Its location is your chest.

Fifth Chakra

This chakra that goes by the term Throat Chakra is located at the bottom of your neck. It is the chakra that enhances your confidence in expressing yourself without fear and it also gives you the ability to communicate clearly and effectively.

Sixth Chakra

This chakra is within your forehead, right between your eyebrows. It is deemed to be located where your pituitary gland is, and is the one that enhances your intuition as well as spiritual awareness.

Seventh Chakra

This chakra that also goes by the reference, Crown Chakra, is on the top area of your head. It is deemed to be located precisely within your pineal gland. This chakra, when working well, is said to liberate your spirit so that you are confident in the choices that you make without being inhibited by prejudices.

Importance of the 6th And 7th Chakras in Opening the Third Eye

Looking at Chakras six and seven, the two chakras that are even close to each other in proximity, you will notice that they are to do with things spiritual. And so, it is safe to say that the two chakras are responsible for the opening and continued activation of your third eye. In fact, that premise is underlined by an expert in these matters, who goes by the name of H.H. Mahatapaswi Shri Kumarswamiji. He asserts that the pituitary as well as the pineal gland must, of necessity, work together to get the third eye well open.

It is worth mentioning that these two chakras are not as restricted as the other five; or rather, they are not zoned in terms of how far and deep their energy flow can affect you. This is because of their nature of dealing with matters of spiritual awareness and intuition. The sixth chakra particularly links up with every one of those other chakras, sending them messages that can influence the way they work.

If you consider, for instance, how the pituitary gland works scientifically, you will notice the influence it has on the physical development of different glands in your body. In fact, it is this great influence over other glands that makes it get the title Master Gland, tiny as it is – pea size, actually. Then when you consider how it influences emotional thoughts, making you appreciate things like music and poetry; and how it helps you formulate intellectual ideas, you will appreciate why it gets the reference, Seat of the Mind.

When again you evaluate the workings of the pineal gland, sitting right in the middle of your brain, you realize how much control it has on matters higher than the physical. It may even be telling the fact that it has a pigment just like the one that exists in your eyes. No wonder it has that control of light over your body. Delving into the state of partnership between these two chakras – your 6th and 7th – and now having a clear idea what power and influence each of them has, you find some kind of moderation that ends up producing the balance attributed to the third eye.

Notice, for example, the influence your 6th chakra has on the development of your other glands. But then again, too much excitement is no good for anyone, whether it is on sensual matters or matters of the heart. And here is where the 7th chakra comes in, inhibiting excess activity of the pituitary – which as you know, is within the 6th chakra. Using a hard fact like the sexual development in an adolescent, as the pituitary gland works towards getting the sex related glands in great shape, the pineal gland is busy ensuring that the adolescent does not experience sexual awakening prematurely.

It is just like the way your sixth chakra, with its power of intuition, gets your thoughts running. Do those thoughts translate instantly and in an automatic manner into action? Well, that is for your seventh chakra to determine. And here lies the balancing act – you have the power of deep and fascinating thoughts, but you also need to evaluate them and see if it is wise to execute them or not. In short, your pineal gland is calling for your introspection in all matters; kind of pulling you magnetically within the illumination of spiritual light. Here you can see the force of intuitive ability as well as a pull towards sobriety, all on the same plane.

Chapter 14:
Increasing the Efficiency of Your 3rd Eye through Clairvoyance

What would you say clairvoyance is? Well, according to the plain English meaning it is that ability to perceive things in an extraordinary way; having a peep into the future which is not equivalent to wishing – rather, some sensory feel of the reality to come.

With reference to the power of the third eye, you are a clairvoyant when you can see something beforehand – meaning a real view of some future happening; see something happening in real time even when you are not close enough to apply your five common senses; and even visualizing something that happened sometime in the past even when you were not privy to it.

Now, have we just said that a clairvoyant can tell the reality pertaining to the past; now; and the future without hearing, seeing, touching, smelling or even feeling? Right! And you may be thinking – those must be the queer looking ladies whose appointments are shrouded in mystery and secrecy; whose fees you pay through the nose. But no – not always... Whereas clairvoyance is a unique practice, it is not because it is a preserve of a few. And clairvoyants need not look weird, scary or funny. Of course, I'll spice it a little bit with some aura of mystery if I'm charging you the services; just to play on your psychology, but really, clairvoyance is something you can also learn, practice and master.

Let us try and understand how the powers of a clairvoyant manifest:

- Having a dream that is vivid and then whatever was in the dream comes to pass.

- Misplacing something you had and then while you are just mum a mental picture of the place you put the thing flashes through your mind – and the thing happened to be right where your mental image took you.

- You could be driving and then you mentally see the actual car you are following turning, say, to the right; and in a minute or so, it literally does so.

- You see someone's image mentally – what sometimes we mistake for 'thinking' about someone; and sometime later in the day that same person gets in touch with you, either in person or via phone or even mail.

Supposing you could do that on all important matters! Yet it is possible for you to enhance the natural power of clairvoyance that you may currently have in your own small way, and be able to visualize things in a more mentally intense manner.

Here are some steps you can take in enhancing your power of clairvoyance:

Abandon your fears

Have you been in a situation where you were so scared of something or someone and had to laugh about it later when you got accustomed to them? I'm imagining being born and brought up on an island where tortoises and turtles were about the only animals you saw. Then one day someone flew you out to the tropics where you saw herds of 4 – 5 meter tall giraffes.

You would think it was not real but a figment of your imagination!

That is the same thing that happens particularly when you are young and you get clairvoyant experiences. If they are scary compared to your situation in real life, you chuck it aside so you will not have to deal with the truth.

- Such is the scenario when a kid has a clairvoyant experience of her or his parents parting ways in a divorce

- A child also shuts out clairvoyant experiences if parents or other adults attribute narrations of such experiences as evil

- A child can also shut out such clairvoyant experiences when mature people fail to believe them and accuse them of lying or having an exaggerated imagination

So what is the reality for the child? The truth is that a child may be born with the third eye clearly open and with clairvoyant abilities very strong, and may, therefore, be seeing his or her spiritual guides very vividly and having clairvoyant experiences with clarity.

How, then, do you rid yourself of this limiting fear?

You can release the fear that inhibits your ability to perceive things as per your natural abilities by affirming your belief in yourself.

- Get a place to sit and make yourself comfortable

- While relaxed, take two or even three long, deep breaths

- As you do the inhaling and exhaling, say something like this: *I'm prepared to let go of all the fear that I have of seeing into the future.*

Be sincere in your questioning

Sometimes you want to use your clairvoyant abilities in a conscious way and so you pose a question to your inner self – be genuine and to the point. It is the only way you are going to receive an answer that is accurate and helpful to you. In short, the reason you are applying your clairvoyance is that you have genuine curiosity and desires. Express them as you feel them.

If, for instance, you are longing to find a romantic partner at a particular party, design your question as precisely as you can, like:

- *Shall I meet a romantic partner at the party tonight? Or:*

- *Shall I get involved with someone romantically tonight?*

The point is to avoid being vague like:

- *I'm I likely to meet someone?*

Think about it this way. If you ask vaguely and get the answer in the affirmative, you could end up meeting a long lost relative or a very interesting comic. Yes! In both cases you will have met someone. But is it the kind of person you are longing for? No. So be to the point and give details as close as you can; otherwise you may end up doubting your clairvoyance while it is your questioning technique that is wanting.

Chapter 15:
Further Enhancement of Your 3rd Eye through Clairvoyance

Do you recall why you are so interested in applying your clairvoyance? It is because you are curious about something you deem important, like the possibility of you linking up with a romantic partner. So, this is what you do to help get clear answers:

Direct your total focus on your third eye

- Sit down and relax

- Direct your focus on your 6th chakra

Sixth... Yes – that chakra that resides just between your eyes and slightly above; between your eyebrows, to be precise. That one is in charge of your high level intuition. That is the position of your third eye, which experts call *Ajna*, and which is known to discharge sharp sensory messages that are clear and telling. As usual, you are taking deep breaths as you concentrate on your third eye – three ins and outs will suffice.

What you are essentially working on is getting this intense energy center that is your 6th chakra to activate your clairvoyance, and hence begin sending psychic images in response to your questions.

And will you get them?

Well, first ascertain that you can see some oval shape (eyelike) at the place where the chakra is supposed to be.

- Now, is that eyelike shape closed?

- Or is it partially open?

- Is it clearly open?

The point is you want that eyelike shape clearly open because that is your third eye, the facilitator of clairvoyance. In case it is not yet open, you need to repeat your affirmation that you are actually prepared to discard all your fears associated with psychic sight; that you are eager to see psychically.

Do you know how you will tell that your third eye has finally opened up besides visualizing it on the oval shape?

You will suddenly enjoy a calming feeling of warm engulfing love.

Take note of the pictures entering your mind

And how do I monitor those pictures, you may be wondering? This is what you need to look out for:

- A picture lingering in your mind in singular – one vivid image

- A picture lingering before your eyes in singular – again one unmistakable picture

- A movie-like image shows within your mind; within your mental arena

- A movie-like image shows before your eyes; beyond your mental arena

And what colors do these pictures come in?

These images do not come in pre-defined colors despite the fact that the third eye is linked to Color Purple or Indigo.

- They sometimes come in plain black and white

- Other times the images come in a full range of colors

- There are times that you see the images in form of cartoons

- Other times you may even see an image in form of a distinct painting

Seek to enhance the brightness as well as the size of your psychic images

How do you do that? Simple: commanding affirmation! With conviction and belief you address your mental pictures in this manner:

My pictures, I direct you to grow in size as well as strength right away!

The idea is to communicate clearly:

- Your unequivocal decision to venture into the realm of the psychic

- Your undivided attention to the emerging images

- Your strong intention to embrace those psychic images

And with that declaration, your pictures become more pronounced – larger; bolder; and even brighter – in a way that is relatively easy to decipher. We have said that this is going to work and it surely should, and you need to believe too that it will.

But supposing there seems to be a hitch with the clarity of the images still not very helpful?

Please note that you will not be the first person to whose first attempt was not exactly yielding. Just do step one in the last chapter once more – releasing all your fears – then proceed as demonstrated. You are bound to get clear readable images that will give you answers to your questions.

Seek interpretation as well as clarification

What is the use of seeing an image if you cannot tell what it represents? Unless you can derive meaning from the pictures that you see in your mind, you will still remain as uninformed as that person with no interest in psychic powers – or even more confused.

Therefore, address the powers in your spiritual world thus:

What is the meaning of these images?

And you can ask that mentally or even verbally, it does not matter. Have faith in your spiritual powers because your guides in the spiritual world are actually intent on helping you; they are normally very co-operative.

Maintain your quiet concentration and you will be rewarded with clear answers in form of:

- Feeling

- Sound

- Thought

Any of those three could be the form in which you get your response.

If you really do not comprehend your answer as communicated, address your spiritual powers and request that you be sent the answers again in a form that you can easily understand.

Maintain your trust

It is just like in your normal day-to-day activities. How can you succeed if you are working with a system that you do not believe in; a system you hardly trust? Impossible! So, in these matters of clairvoyance, doubting the strength or credibility of the psychic system is sure self-sabotage. You must trust what you are working with – your psychic ability; your clairvoyance; your ability to get answers pertaining to your future. It is absolutely crucial that you believe and trust in the clairvoyant images that you receive too. That way, they are going to work as expected as there are no conflicting energies.

Chapter 16:
Purifying and Activating Your Third Eye

What aspect of your third eye needs purifying?

Well, you need first of all to remember the fact that everyone has the third eye whether they know it or not; or whether they acknowledge it or not. The thing is that for some people, the third eye is almost dormant. And that is only because they have not been making good use of it or they have not been leading what can be termed exactly healthy lives. Do not forget that the pineal gland, that tiny endocrine gland that is within your vertebrae brain exists in everyone. And it is the one that plays link between the world you see physically and feel, and the ethereal and astral planes – the reason it gets the third eye reference.

What precisely causes the third eye to close without warning?

As has been indicated before, this closing of the third eye has mainly to do with lifestyle. And so by the age of seventeen, most people do not have an active third eye worth writing home about and they lead their lives with emotional upheavals, unnecessary anxieties and lots of other emotional and spiritual imbalances. A physical check will reveal heavy calcification of this area, with an MRI indicating a clear calcium lump.

Lifestyle factors causing calcification of the pineal gland:

- Toxins consumed through modern day foods or even imbibed from the environment

- Excessive fluoride gotten from toothpaste or even some drinking water

- Hormones consumed through processed foods

- Additives contained in processed foods

- Excess sugars consumed

- Consumption of artificial sweeteners

Why care about an inactive third eye?

Can you visualize someone who is pessimistic and living without hope – someone who does not believe that anyone can be good to them and one who has no inclination to do any good to anyone? That is actually the image of a person whose third eye is far from active. In Hindu, a third eye that is closed goes by the reference, *Anja Chakra*.

How bad can a closed third eye be?

Well, terribly bad. Think of:

- Someone living in some kind of confusion

- Leading a life full of uncertainty

- Finding yourself being ever cynical

- Pessimism being kind of your middle name

- A tendency to be overly jealous and envious

- Being single sided in outlook

These are some of the bad effects of having your third eye inactive, and of course, you are yet to mention the more subtle effects including poor sleeping patterns, bad moods and such, which are caused by undersupply of the melatonin hormone, that derivative of serotonin. And there is the poor co-ordination between your left and right hemispheres of your brain. Let us just say that with your third eye barely open, a lot can go wrong physically, emotionally as well as spiritually. In fact, whatever an active third eye makes good, an inactive third eye is bound to affect negatively. And considering how closely your pineal gland works with your hypothalamus gland, a defective pineal gland is bound to adversely affect different body rhythms. These include:

- How and when you experience thirst and how it affects you

- How and when you experience hunger and how it affects you

- How you experience sexual desire and how you handle it

- How your biological clock works, including how your aging process goes

So much for what goes wrong when your third eye is almost closed. How about when you have an active third eye? What do you exactly stand to gain?

- You see things and evaluate issues and situations with clarity

- You have high concentration whatever you are dealing with

- You are pretty good at perspicuity

- You find yourself experiencing bliss

- You are highly intuitive

- You find it easy to make decisions

- You have great insight into issues

- Your dreams are vivid and you are comfortable in your lucid dreaming

- You are fine engaging in astral projection

- Definitely, you experience high quality sleep

- Your imagination is highly enhanced

- You are able to see or visualize things with your physical eyes closed

- You can clearly feel your spiritual energy flowing

- You are able to see spiritual beings and see things on higher planes

- You are able to appreciate your energy presence as well as your open communication channels

That is why you need your pineal gland open, that gateway to your higher self, the source of your intuition and peace; and the source of harmony between you and your environment.

<u>How do you keep your third eye open or open that which is closed?</u>

By avoiding excessive fluoride

Drinking or cooking with tap water can lead to consumption of fluoride in excessive quantities. Is that all for overconsumption of fluoride? Of course, it is not. There are so many other ways you can get excessive fluoride in your body that cutting them off all of a sudden may feel too drastic. For that matter, it may be advisable to take a gradual route to reducing your fluoride intake.

Here is an alert of other ways your body gets excessive fluoride:

- Eating fruits that are not organic

- Also eating inorganic vegetables

- Eating red meat

- Drinking sodas

- Consuming artificial drinks

Basically why consumption of sodas and artificial drinks gives you excessive fluoride is just the water with which they are usually made – quite impure. And do not think that taking your showers without a filter is safe either.

Use of a pineal gland detoxifier or even a stimulant

There are various natural products – some of them extracts – that you can use either to stimulate your pineal gland or outright detoxify it. This will ensure that energy flow within your sixth chakra is flowing well and there is balance in your energy vibrations. That way, whatever physical, mental or spiritual functions are supported by your pineal gland will go on exemplary well. Likewise, you will cease to have the distractions that usually come with a blocked sixth chakra. The ingredients you could reach out to for the purpose of detoxifying your third eye include:

Hydrilla verticillata,	Blue-green algae	Ginseng	chlorophyll
Chlorella	Iodine	Borax	blue skate liver oil
Spirulina	Zeolite	bentonite clay	D3

Including in your meals foods containing detoxifying ingredients such as:

Raw cacao	Water Melon	Seaweed	Hemp seeds
Goji berries	Bananas	Noni juice	Coconut oil
Garlic	Honey	Cilantro	
Lemon (and other foods with citric acid)	Raw apple cider vinegar (and any other foods with malic acid)		

Are you possibly wondering how to consume the apple cider vinegar in its raw state? Well, here is something you might wish to try:

- Get yourself some purified water

- Get some raw honey – 2 tablespoons are sufficient

- Now your apple cider vinegar – 8 tablespoons are good enough

Now mix those ingredients and enjoy your drink. Regular consumption of this self-made drink will bring back your health in no time and you will find yourself loving your life more than ever before.

Getting into the habit of using essential oils

This point does not need belaboring, of course, seeing there is a whole chapter on essential oils and how well they support your third eye. As long as you are using essential oils and particularly those that go well with the sixth chakra, you can be sure your pineal gland will remain stimulated. And, of course, you know when your third eye is working optimally you are great at:

- Enhanced spiritual awareness

- Great ability to meditate

- Smooth, stable and fruitful astral projection

- Everything to do with mental and spiritual health

What are some of those essential oils recommended for stimulation of the pineal gland?

They include:

Lavender	Frankincense	Davana	Pink Lotus
Sandalwood	Parsley	Pine	Mugwort

What is the most effective way of using essential oils?

Well, you have choices. According to the time you want to use your oil, the environment, or mere preference, you can opt for any of the following methods:

- Burning the oil in a diffuser

- Having the oil in a nebulizer

- Adding the oil to your bath water

- Simply inhaling the scent of the essential oil

Caution:

Just be sure you are not inhaling too much of Mugwort or inhaling it too regularly as it is known to produce neurotoxins at some point and those are not great for your health.

Sungazing

Well, the sun is not only great for solar power – it is also great for mental and spiritual power. Making it a habit of watching it directly immediately it rises in the morning for about 15 minutes, and then watching it again as it finally sets in the evening for some further 15 minutes, is a great way of boosting the function of your pineal gland.

Meditating and regular chanting

Did you know that chanting had some impact on your physical being? Apart from the obvious exercising of your vocal chords that has nothing to do with your third eye, chanting also makes some bone – the tetrahedron – within your nose to literally resonate. This resonating is the one that then causes the much needed stimulation of your pineal gland. Sounds magical!

Yet, there is a physiological explanation for that. Once your pineal gland is stimulated:

- It begins to secrete some hormone that is credited with keeping you looking younger

- It begins to instigate some hormonal balance in your body

In fact, the chanting has a direct impact on your third eye too, particularly when you consider its link with your fourth chakra. If you recall, the fourth chakra is around the area of your heart – the reason it is referred to as Seat of Love; unconditional love, actually. Now when you chant 'OM', you begin to be cosmically aware; you begin to have a universal outlook to things.

How long should the chanting go?

Well, chanting for a session of 5 minutes up to, say, 10 minutes is good enough. Of course, there is no overdose as in the case of inhaling the Mugwort essence. When it comes to chanting, you can go on as long as you wish and as long as you are comfortable doing it.

Using natural crystals

There is, of course, a full chapter in this book dedicated to the use of crystals for the purpose of opening your third eye, but it helps to add some things that you can do with crystals to stimulate a sluggish third eye. Let us begin by pointing out that not every rock you come across is apt to stimulate your third eye. There are particular ones with that capability, and mostly they bear colors that are relevant to your brow and even the crown chakras. The colors you need to look out for are mainly indigo; violet; and also dark purple.

Remember when analyzing how well your third eye is working you have to consider, not just how well your pineal gland is working, but also how well your pituitary is working. So both the 6th and the 7th chakras are really crucial.

Here are specific crystals that are great at stimulating your pineal gland:

- The wand form of amethyst

- The wand form of the laser quartz

- The moonstone

- The pertersite

- The purple colored sapphire

- The purple colored violet tourmaline

- The rhodonite

- The rose aura quartz

- The sodalite crystal

What is the most effective way of using the stimulating crystals?

Well, there are various places you could place your crystals, including wearing them as ornaments, but for the purpose of stimulating your third eye, the best choices would be:

- Placing your selected crystal directly on top of your brow chakra, the presumed location of your third eye

Note that a stimulating crystal is not something that you just place on your brow for a second or two and then remove, nor is it something that you stick on your brow for days on end. The ideal duration is between 15min – 30min and that is every day or on alternate days.

- Taking your crystal wand, whichever it is, and pointing it at your third eye.

And mark you the tip of the wand must literally touch the skin of your body. In this position, look up at the sun but with closed eyes. For this exercise, a 5min – 10min duration on a daily basis is sufficient.

When you do that, you get the rays of the sun penetrating through the base of your crystal wand and goes on to beam right into your pineal gland. And that is how your pineal gland gets stimulated.

It is important to note that if your chosen crystal is quartz, either as a wand or otherwise, its benefits go beyond stimulating your third eye. In fact, it is safe to say that all your chakras stand to benefit from the use of quartz crystals.

Massaging using magnets

What you do here is stick your magnet onto the skin just above your brow using an adhesive tape. That is how you will get your pineal gland decalcified and your third eye stimulated.

How long or regular should this exercise be?

This exercise, like the others, need not take very long. For stimulation by magnet, a couple of hours each day are sufficient. And you should do it in the day when you have a chance of finding sunshine, and never on your head when you are about to fall asleep.

Magnets help by influencing your body to alkalinity; particularly on the area where the magnet is actually attached to your body. And as for their strength, they do get a boost from the sun's energy.

Of the eight stimulating methods explained above, which is the best?

Well, all these methods of stimulating your third eye are great. What you could do is either to make a choice of one, or get a few and use them alternately in a kind of regular manner. Once you begin with the third eye stimulation process, commitment and dedication are key factors to success. So you need to make your exercises or procedures regular.

Chapter 17:
Activating Your 3rd Eye through Simple Exercises

Are you waiting for the day you have your third eye fully open in order to begin maintaining it? Well, that is not the way to go. The extent to which your third eye is open notwithstanding, you need to do certain things to ensure that the energy of your sixth chakra is balanced. Even when you have not reached the heightened awareness levels where astral travels are normal to you, there is still the normal sixth sense that everyone speaks about. That too is part of the third eye business. In fact, it is the reason many people know the brow chakra as the psychic chakra.

Of course, once you have increased your awareness and you are enjoying much higher levels of intuition, you appreciate more the need to take care of your pineal gland, which is actually a representation of your third eye. Just to recap, here are some of the success factors the third eye is credited with:

- Being the originator of your inner vision

- Being responsible for your psychic visions

- Being responsible for your clairvoyance

- Being responsible for your astral travels

- Being responsible for precognition

- On the overall, linking your physical world to that which is of a spiritual nature

Since you want your third eye active, which means you do not wish your pineal gland to be calcified; atrophied; or plainly dormant, here are things you need to practice:

Visualizing

This is a great way to keep your third eye open. It is actually known to begin the energy flow between your mind and your own physical body. This is how you go about visualization:

- You first of all find a place that is quiet and just relax. Your relaxing position may be lying down or even sitting in the so called lotus position.

- The next thing is to close your two physical eyes and to allow your mind to clear. Of course it is not going to be necessarily easy to get rid of all your thoughts in one go, so this is something you need to understand that this is a gradual process – allowing worries and concerns to fade away possibly one at a time.

- Once you register calmness in your mind, it is time to begin directing your mental energy towards your pineal gland. And so you begin to focus on your brow, that position of your third eye. Very likely, once you have done that effectively, you are going to feel some warm sensation around that area, and sometimes what you feel is a tingling sensation.

- At this juncture, you need to actually visualize your third eye right on your forehead, and get yourself visualizing images of it opening. Then with a smooth flow, feel the energy of that third eye falling into sync with the energies from the rest of your body.

- Once you have managed this successfully, you are done. Now it is for you to keep repeating this exercise, step by step, until you are satisfied you have reached the full potential of your third eye.

To check how well you are doing with your third eye, try a simple exercise where you relax and close your eyes; then you try and see the room you are in from your third eye. If when you open your eyes, everything you see is the same way you saw it with your eyes closed, then you know you are on the right track. Later you may try entering another room and having a quick glance and then closing your eyes to see what you can see with your third eye. As you proceed with these exercises, you will become more and more confident in the workings of your third eye. And you will, definitely, keep your third eye stimulated and in good shape.

First Awakening

Here you need to be ready to make a chant of the term, 'thoh', which in actual fact you pronounce as 'toe'. Any specific style of chanting...? Yes – a specific vibration that falls between high pitched and deep tone. Try to hit that within the range of alto. Of course you are not expected to think of the musical notes or something like that but rather to go by your feel. If you like how you feel about your tone, then you have likely hit the right note. So stop second guessing yourself and get on with business. Here is one of those times you are encouraged to trust your personal instincts.

What you need to take seriously now is the regularity with which you conduct this chanting exercise. You need to religiously do this after every 24hrs until you have done it for three good days. From then on, you can be assured you are one of those advantaged people with an active third eye.

Do you know the practical bit of this exercise beyond the chant?

Well, you are not going to do your chant while writing notes or making coffee – no! When it comes to opening your third eye or stimulating it, you need to be in the right environment otherwise the flow of energies and matching of their frequencies is not going to go right. As such, you need to follow the following steps in the procedure of Awakening One:

- Sit down as you have your back in an upright position.

- Once you feel you are properly seated, take in air deeply and hold it till you can hold it no more. In short, you will be holding your breath as long as you are comfortable doing it.

- Now let your jaws open leaving some little space between your upper and lower teeth.

- You now need to direct the tip of your tongue into that little space between your upper and lower jaw.

- Of course not much of your tongue will pass, the reason you are dealing with the tip. What you need to do is to have that tip of the tongue feel some pressure from your teeth. So the space is small but the tip of your tongue is kind of trying to push through. Essentially what you are trying to achieve is equivalent to producing the sound of, 'TH' from the English article, 'the'.

- Of course hear you are not interested in pronouncing the word, the, but producing some vibrations that will send signals to your third eye. So once you are set with your tongue tip in the right place, you begin to release air through your mouth. Make it one gradual and relatively long exhalation. As air pushes out against your teeth and tongue, you will feel it and at the same time hear yourself producing the sound, *T-H-H-O-H-H*.

What should you expect to feel in order to know you are getting things working right?

Simple – a clear sensation within your jaws and the area of your cheeks. At the same time, you will feel the tone of the sound created by passing air resonating in the area of your third eye. Once you have achieved this, you know you have succeeded. But that should not be the end of the story for this first awakening.

So what next...?

Make a repeat of that exercise till you have hit 5 good times – and that is consecutively. Now you are fine.

Second Awakening

You can aptly call this a sequel to Awakening One. However, this second stage makes you feel so good that you may be tempted to keep doing it. But you surely do not want to open gates you cannot close or get yourself overwhelmed with an over-active third eye. So, do the second awakening exercises just once in a week – no more. And, in fact, you are advised not to even contemplate involving yourself with Awakening Two before 10days have lapsed after your Awakening One. In actual fact, the recommended interval is from 10 – 14 days.

And why is that break necessary?

Well, you need to take a break from such intense activities as those related to third eye activation or stimulation so that you can adapt to your new status of awareness. And, of course, your energy flow and vibrations will have become part of you as you begin the next stage which is Awakening Two.

How to go about the euphoric exercises of Awakening Two:

- Begin by inhaling air deeply and then holding that breathe for a span lasting five counts; then exhale.

- Repeat that breathing in and out three consecutive times. The essence of this part of exercising is to get you fully relaxed and also focused.

- It is now the ideal moment to shift your focus to the location of your third eye; and you know where that is – the brow. So you focus on that spot between your eyes until you begin to register some sensation like the one you felt in Awakening One. You may even feel some form of slight pressure around there. And most importantly, you will be well aware and conscious of that spot that is the location of your third eye.

- Now take in air as in a deep inhalation the way you did in Awakening One, and hold that breathe similarly as long as you find it comfortable for you. This time round exhale slowly through your mouth as you verbalize the term 'May'. So what you are doing here is kind of mentioning the 5th month of the year in a pretty slow and gradual style – and in the alto tone.

- Do this inhalation and exhalation till you have completed five times.

- Are you just gaping into space as you inhale and exhale? Of course not – not an empty gaze, at least. You will be concentrating on the energy flow through your head as you vibrate the term 'May, and feel it as it touches the area of your brow chakra. Then you follow it calmly as that energy enters your brain where your pineal gland is and up to the location of your crown chakra.

So that is precisely what you do. Now, how do you feel?

Well, you cannot be quiet in full concentration, repeatedly vibrate the same term – May – from a flow of exhaled air, and yet cease to have some noticeable experience. So here is what you should expect to experience:

- You may feel kind of light on the overall

- You could have a significant feel of energy flow

- You may experience a tingling sensation within your head

- You may even feel some kind of pressure within the area of your crown chakra

- There are even instances when you get to experience intense euphoria

And what is the timing of this experience?

Well, you cannot say it is five or so hours after you are through with your second awakening or even days or this number of days thereafter. The fact is that you can experience those sensations just hours after your exercising or even a couple of days from then.

When, thereafter, do those feelings disappear?

In actual fact, they do not. Once your third eye has been set in motion and is working optimally, the feeling of spiritual energy flow; the slight pressure around your crown area; and the rest of it could easily become a permanent experience for you. And if you want to know how beneficial that is, look at the following advantages:

- You will find it relatively easy to practice void meditation

- Your level of clairvoyance will be elevated

- You will find it relatively easy to develop psychic abilities

- You will find it relatively easy to sharpen any psychic abilities you already have

- Any attempt at developing and activating your paranormal senses will be much more fruitful than otherwise.

Chapter 18:
Benefits of the Third Eye

Do you now see how different you would be with the power of the third eye? From what we have seen so far, there is a way you can empty your fears and anxieties from your system and replace them with the tranquility that comes with awareness. And what a peaceful world you would find despite the ups and downs of everyday life! In simple terms, you do not feel at peace with the world because people stop quarreling and nations cease hostilities – no. It is the awareness of what is going on around you, and your appreciation of your abilities and limitations that gives you peace. You surely do not want to miss the chance to lead a relaxed life after understanding the potential you have with the third eye.

Let us summarize the benefits of opening your third eye:

You will begin to be aware of things unseen and things unheard

When you have your third eye open, you get to be conscious of things that are happening distance away from you, and after a period of getting used to, you know when that awareness calls for action. So you can find yourself making a telephone call in the middle of the night to check on someone, not because you have had a bad dream, but because you have gotten insight into some bad experience the person is having. In short, you get to live your life with a kind of spiritual guide.

You become in charge of your life

The intuition that comes with opening of your third eye becomes like some natural wisdom. You are able to turn left and lead others in that direction when you sense danger on the right. And because of that kind of reliable sense of direction, others cannot help but respect you. To them, what they see and sense in you is a kind of admirable maturity for what you say is well thought out, and it ends up guiding you to a much better place than otherwise. With this kind of ability to control your life, walking away from danger and walking towards opportunities becomes like second nature to you. When others seek to pay a fortune to get their lives deciphered by a psychic, you just smile knowing quite well you would not need to pay anyone to do what you can do for yourself.

It harnesses your intuitive wisdom and in the process transforms your life

Through the various techniques of keeping your third eye open, you end up with improved self awareness; controlled emotions; and ability to keep stress levels low. This gives your life great harmony, something that is elusive in many people's lives.

Increased ability to discover hidden passions

When you have heightened awareness of you as part of a complex environment, with the ability to adjust yourself to suit different situations, thanks to the third eye, you have a better chance to ignite fresh passions that you never knew you had. For the passions that you were already pursuing, you will find yourself doing far much better than before. You will appreciate that better if you think of a situation where, instead of worrying all day long about your pending bills, you find yourself coming up with intelligent ways of managing your debts.

You find yourself with no propensity to absorb negative thoughts

This is how this happens: during your third eye opening sessions, you allow your senses to see your inside. And as you take deep breaths in and out, you do not just acknowledge the good thoughts but also those that are not so pleasant. Simply put, you do not take, for instance, meditation exercises, in order to escape reality – no. You do so in order that you can appreciate the thoughts going through your mind, and subsequently let the negative thoughts leave. Negative thoughts do not thrive in an environment that is clear and peaceful – they dwell in toxic environments. What now guides you is the intuitive wisdom that fills your mind, which then gives you much needed patience to handle the not-so-pleasant things in your life.

You get to learn things you never thought yourself capable of

This is because in sessions of meditation, you are able to hear sounds and visualize things that are not within your vicinity, and you also get to feel emotions you would normally not sense as a person whose third eye is closed.

In the process, you are able to handle relatively well people who are stressed out and people who are annoying. You are able to accommodate their unpleasant state without becoming victim of their negative vibrations because of your intuition and patience. In short, having your third eye active is a great way of keeping free of unnecessary pressure and also free of anxiety.

You are able to look deep inside you, which makes you appreciate the outside all the more

It is at the time of meditation that you get to open up to your deepest passions, and this puts you in a good position to adjust your daily life accordingly. In short, what you discover in your inside manifests on your physical life. For instance, if you are at peace with yourself after meditation, you hardly get uncontrolled temptations to shout at people – you are patient. And if you have found your passion, you set your life goals in a decisive way – you get focused.

Chapter 19:
How about opening your 3rd Eye in unconventional ways?

Well, the norm feels safe and sure, and it is more often stress free, but hey! How about venturing outside the usual; the norm; the conventional? It sounds like a little adventure, and there is, really, nothing wrong with having some fun while trying to reach the realms of the highly spiritual or highly intuitive. In fact, the reality is that the norm can sometimes be boring – or not so much enticing. Of course we need to mention here that whatever you do in a bid to open your third eye needs to be done within the tenets of moderation and good health.

With that in mind, let us look at some crazy sounding methods, but which ultimately end up opening your 3rd eye in ways unknown to you before:

Searching for the Poetic Dragon Smoke

Here, you are being called upon to make a great leap from what you know and what you have always believed, to a mental sphere where you are ready to register new things. You will be accepting to break the boundary markers of the finite, and allowing your mind to venture into the world of the infinite. In short, you will refuse to see things at face value, but instead get your mind reading between the lines with the openness to embrace new meanings and perspectives. Allow yourself some mental adventure and let your third eye embrace the great mystery.

This is exemplified well in the way ancient poets laid their work. They would write things that are familiar to you in an interesting way, but then in the middle of their work they would, sort of, lose you. They would write things with pretty deep meaning, and which would call for great intellect for you to comprehend. And then they would end up resuming their initial simplicity and tone. According to the Chinese, those poets were riding on dragons and during the span that they lose you in their writing, it is the time their dragons are emitting smoke, the way it happens in major Chinese festivities; and in the process shooting the poet to the world unknown – the unconscious. Of course, the poets would later resume the common world and we begin to read something familiar. Seeking to open your third eye is an attempt to cross the bridge of the familiar to step into the arena of the unfamiliar; the apparently mystical.

Unbecoming everything

You see, we know you as this or that. You could be the medical doctor who is very good in mathematics and science – full stop. Or you could be the great soprano singer. Now while those statements sound complimentary, do you not see some danger in them becoming limiting? And it may be one aspect that puts pressure on you to remain as we know you. If we know you as a great mathematician and scientist, we kind of close your doors to the world of art. It is like you have got to sneak to attend a writers' congress because we do not expect you to do well in it.

However, if you erase those limiting parameters and allow yourself to be what you are yet to know, you will be opening your third eye and giving yourself opportunity to explore deep and wide. And remember it is not just other people who limit you. In fact, you are your own greatest limiting factor. And you are the only one who can liberate yourself from static limitations, to the realm of uninhibited thinking.

You will let your third eye open up by clearing the self conflict you constantly experience – the conflict of fearing to lose what you have, for example, without being sure that you will have something worthwhile to replace it. Come to think of it – how can you ever add anything into your hand if it is always secured in a tight grip? Liberate yourself from society and then use the conflict within you to undergo a process of self regeneration – that is the advice from Jennifer Ratna-Rosenhagen, the renowned US professor of History who is also an author.

By taking this route of undoing things that are said to make you, it is important that you take into consideration the possibility of not becoming something in particular. In short, you are not striving to free yourself from limitations only to jump into a different form of limitation – no. Embrace the idea of setting yourself free with a view to becoming everything possible; being the authentic you. The fact is that you are a multi-layered individual with diverse and exceptional potential. Let your third eye open your vision to those avenues.

Using apocalyptic glasses to see

Just as Rumi, the Persian poet of the 13th century, said, whatever you see or observe has its real roots in the world of the unseen. And for you to be able to follow those roots, you need to look through those far reaching lenses. You get to see the truth that exists but we do not see owing to our set beliefs and our perceptions.

Sometimes we are blinded to our potential by where we find ourselves particularly when we are born. This is referred to as *caught-reality*. Of course there are perceptions we develop because of what we are taught. It could be in school, by our parents, and so on. This way of looking at things is referred to as *taught-reality*. Then there is the universe that is bigger than us, and with nature doing its thing without referring to anyone for an opinion. It also has a way of influencing our perceptions. This is what is referred to as *ought-reality*. With all these dimensions that are not necessarily in harmony, we seek to understand them all as a package. What we end up perceiving is the *sought-reality*.

If you have clearly followed this method of opening your 3rd eye, you will appreciate that the apocalyptic glasses are not giving you any specific direction to follow. What it does is just help in opening your third eye so that you are able to see what you are capable of learning and perceiving without external influences. The apocalyptic glasses are, in effect, immanently a plain white, where they show you neither colorful optimism nor dull pessimism.

Practicing Counter-weltanschauung dynamics

Do not worry about the German jargon. All that the long word, *weltanschauung*, means is *worldview*. You realize that a lot of what you do and what you aim to achieve has its benchmark on the outlook the world gives you about things. But the suggestion here is: try and ignore those world benchmarks and look at things from contrasting viewpoints. See what you come up with.

Inevitably, if you go all out to do that, you will find your third eye opening, and you begin critically evaluating your situation and your contentions. And you will begin to appreciate the world from an open-minded perspective. What essentially this method seeks to achieve is a state of mind that is as open and as authentic as nature itself.

Practicing faux pas dynamics

Well, the idea is not really to go being rude to people, but it is just to develop some carefree attitude of a kind, such that you are not uptight at the thought of going wrong a decimal. Acknowledge deep down you that the world is not stable in anything. As such, circumstances that create a state of happiness in your life are not necessarily eternal. Likewise, those that create an unhappy state are not eternal either. The lesson, therefore, is that you prepare yourself for any eventuality.

Riding on the same wave, when you are succeeding and others seem to be failing, do not be haughty and contemptuous. Be good to them and be sincere about it – not patronizing. You will find yourself experiencing some double jointed spirituality; giving you a pleasant balance. Yet even with that nice feeling, you ought not to revel too much on your successful life lest you slip. Remember pride is what precedes a fall.

In summary, we are saying that it is alright to laugh at everything, good or bad, and even ridiculing what others take to be untouchable. Whereas that tendency keeps the powerful people around in check, it also opens and keeps open your third eye.

Practicing crazy wisdom

Here what you are trying to visualize is your soul. You are seeking some package of wisdom or some software that can connect you to the world of mystery. The third eye is actually the interface you are seeking so that you can understand that mystery that nobody can solve. In fact, that is the analogy of the famous novelist and poet, Tom Robbins.

In this crazy wisdom, one way of opening your third eye is trying to be the effective link between youth and adulthood. So, somehow, you get to become this beginner who is eager and open to learning, and that mature person who is full of wisdom. You will be that person that is neither a fool per se, and nor a wise person. In essence, you will be ready to critic what others take to be ideal, and you will seek to dismantle and analyze the beliefs of a pragmatist.

This is not madness – not in the least. What is it then? Critiquing a pragmatist the same way you critic an idealist? Yes; there is good reason for that. Appreciate that pragmatism and idealism can go hand in hand. Pragmatism keeps you grounded while idealism keeps your vision alive. With that marriage of perspectives, you will open your third eye, embrace fresh ideas that pragmatists would otherwise smother, and then implement them in a realistic way, contrary to the way idealists do – getting lost in fantasy. In summary, this crazy wisdom of yours will widen your paradigm, and you will begin to be creative in thinking and deed. And it is no secret, really, that you need to be creative in order to emerge a genius. And that tells you how much more creative you need to be if you are to appreciate the world of mystery.

Chapter 20:
Seven Things You Can Do To Sharpen Your Psychic Abilities

Did we mention that you could be as good as anyone else in matters psychic if only you were for it wholesomely? What that simply implies is that you do not inhibit your potential to see into the non-physical world by ignoring your elevated intuition.

In short, try to open up to the idea of higher powers; the power to receive extra-ordinary communication. Remember you may be an ordinary mortal but you are more than a physical body – you have your spiritual element, and it is very active in you. The onus is on you to let that spiritual element manifest itself in your life; in the way you see and interpret things. Avoid selling yourself short as the spiritual world is universal and not for a select few.

You can develop and perfect your spiritual skills if you so wish. And why not, anyway, considering what power you have when you have a good idea which way is potentially good for you and which one is potentially disastrous?

To be a great clairvoyant, one with the third eye clearly open, you need to be consistently at peace with yourself. You also need to keep meditating in order to keep your psychic abilities sharp and strong.

On the overall, however, this is what you can do to sharpen your psychic abilities:

Refuse to embrace any negative thoughts

You are being reminded here that just like the city of Rome was not built in a single day, so will it take you sometime to hone your psychic skills unless you are one of those born intensely psychic.

- Trust that you have the psychic power within you even when you are yet to prove it in action

- Reading on other people's journeys and especially those who began practicing clairvoyance in adult life

- Try to emulate those who at one time felt as frustrated as you sometimes feel and do what do the exercises they did to hone their skills

- Embrace every spiritual experience you undergo however trivial it may seem and that will keep you inspired

- Always stay hopeful and keep trying

Set time aside solely to relax and meditate

So what is it with meditation? For one, you cannot meditate unless you are physically and mentally at ease. So we are saying that you need to consciously set sometime aside to sit and be at peace with your whole self. And this is how your meditation will help sharpen your psychic abilities:

- You are practically concentrating on zero and so your mind will be clear of thoughts

- You will be taking slow deep breaths and your metabolic rate will drop

- Your body will cease to be tense and energy will flow better within you

- The pattern of your brain waves will significantly change in a manner to enhance your mental performance

- In summary, getting in touch with your spiritual side, that one that enhances your intuition and clairvoyance will be relatively easy.

Be at peace with your neighbors

Here you are not being referred to the people on either side of your fence – no. You are being referred to people with whom you interact on a day-to-day basis. Can we summarize here that you are not to going to go far in your psychic endeavors if your life is full of drama?

- To the best of your ability, avoiding conflict is a suitable move

- If you find yourself in the mix of it, try your best to resolve the issue – constructively, that is.

- Make your every argument as constructive as you can

Avoid abusing your psychic abilities

Just as Wiccans say, mess someone up and that mess backfires on you threefold. In this case, you simply are not going to go through opening your third eye to see what you are morally or religiously not supposed to see (whatever your religion is!) Your mind will be so conflicted as you try to do it that no positive energy will flow through to help you bring the psychic images that you wish for. The power of psychic abilities lies in the strong and steady flow of positive energy – not the negative one. And if you try to abuse these spiritually superior abilities, guilt will, no doubt, invade your soul, and you will jeopardize any chances you ever had of sharpening your psychic abilities further.

Try some psychometric exercises

In psychometrics, what you do is to learn something concerning someone or even an event by simply having a feel with your hands of some inanimate object.

So you may wish to touch something like a chair and hope to learn some history from it. If you succeed, you may begin to see in a psychic way someone who used to sit on the chair – maybe a leader of sorts; a beautiful child; something interesting. However, having in mind that you are trying to enhance your psychic abilities and not to bog your mind down with stressful learning exercises, try not to put too much pressure on yourself. Basically:

- Do not, under any circumstances, try to force any psychic images. You need to let the image coming across, if any, to do so naturally.

- Avoid stressing yourself. If no image is forthcoming, give it a rest

- Avoid the feeling of exasperation – it is hardly helpful

- Remember it is fine to feel nothing about such an inanimate object. Who says that every object has a story worth analyzing, anyway?

Sharpening your abilities in remote viewing

Here we are talking of honing your skills in seeing things on your astral plane. Heard of it? You do not just see these things, really, but you actually travel to some other place while leaving your physical body behind; and you can do all the exploration that you wish where you have visited. This is referred to as astral projection, and mastering it is a sure way of sharpening your psychic abilities.

- Once you set your mind onto that astral or spiritual journey, see as much as you can at your target destination – a place you can check out the day that follows

- When you actually visit that place, say the following day, observe if the items you saw and the colors you saw on your astral travel earlier on are there for real

If they correspond, you will be assured your psychic abilities are getting sharper.

Embark on enhancing your powers of telepathy

Can you imagine how much concentration you need to be able to tell something in a telepathic way? Very intense, indeed – yet it is a good tool to enhance your psychic abilities. Small frequent exercises are helpful; such as:

- Asking a friend to roll a dice in hiding and letting you tell the side that is facing up

- Asking a friend to draw a card from a deck of cards and then you try to tell which card it actually is – spades; diamonds; and such.

- Trying to make a guess on what someone you trust is thinking

Of course, you could do such exercises a hundred and one times before you get it right even once, but hey – if you are really trying to concentrate and focus, that is what matters. Sooner or later your psychic energy system is going to open up and you are going to find it easier to nail these things.

Chapter 21:
How to Become a Psychic Medium

We have already learnt in this book that a medium is able to link personal energies with others beyond the physical realm, including those of spirits of people who have passed on. What we may not have learnt is that psychic mediums use various means to tap higher information, including palmistry; psychometrics; and even readings or tarot cards as well as crystal balls.

In order to sharpen your abilities as a psychic medium, it is important that you appreciate first the level of your aptitude.

Appreciate when it is you that can pass for a psychic medium

You have got to be able to communicate with spirits on other planes by clairvoyance; clairaudience; and even Clairsentience.

Understand if you are a natural psychic medium or you just have a deep interest in being one

Whatever you are, it is important to identify your strongest abilities amongst clairvoyance; clairaudience; and clairsentience.

Read about the experiences of different psychic mediums

You can easily identify with the abilities of other practicing mediums and get inspiration from them. And even as you strive to learn from others, you need to be ware of fake mediums and give them a wide berth.

Commit to sharpening your spiritual awareness

Paying attention to your intuition helps as you are able to identify those urges that you may describe as odd but also accompanied by strong energies. Here, it is important that you do not dismiss any dreams that you may experience.

You need to spare sometime in the morning to enjoy some quiet time, where you allow any superior emotions to overwhelm you. This is the ideal time to receive communication from energies from higher realms.

You may also wish to have a go at free writing

This is where you write things communicated to you from outside realms without you consciously thinking about it. Do not worry if you find those writings not being clear. Over time, you will be able to decipher the meaning in their patterns.

Begin to make deliberate efforts to communicate with spirits

At this juncture, it is advisable to work with other psychic mediums – within a mediumship circle – where you learn the best settings for this kind of exercise. Basically what you need to be able to receive messages from higher realms is:

- A quiet room

- A room with dimmed lights

- Some lit candles within the room

- Ability to chant a prayer in preparation for spiritual communication

- Ability to appreciate the presence of spirits in the room

- Ability to perceive messages; images; smells; feelings; and even words delivered by the spirits

- Ability and boldness to ask the spirits to identify themselves and you confirming it aloud

It may help to take a course in mediumship

You can undertake such learning by reading various books by experts; attending psychic fairs; attending psychic conferences and workshops; or even taking online courses.

Begin to practice your psychic abilities on other people

If you identify a person who still has unresolved issues with a relative or a friend who has passed on, try and work with them and be the link between that person and the spirit of the departed. As you try to understand messages from such spirits and as you also try to convey messages from the living to the spirits of the departed, you will be honing your skills and building your confidence too.

If you want to learn the right way:

- Minimize the details you seek about the departed

- Do not even inquire into the name of the deceased

- Do not inquire about the person's birth date

- Do not inquire into the person's physique

If without making those personal inquiries you are able to come up with the right attributes of the deceased, then you know you are on the right track, and that you are doing well as a psychic medium.

Get set for emotional experiences

Be ready to undergo a relatively emotional process when linking up people with spirits in the other realm of the departed; and be ready to deal with an emotional consultant as well. However, soon you will be somewhat hardened and will not feel the pressure of a very emotional experience.

You may consider establishing an enterprise as a psychic medium

The more you attend to clients, the more you gain experience and the more you hone your skills as a medium.

- Have in mind that there are laws to be followed in every country and you need to adhere to them in case you begin making money out of your psychic abilities.

- There are different business models that you could use, but it would help to consult other psychic mediums for advice.

Be Ware

- As a psychic medium, there are chances of you being wrong in either delivering your messages or even receiving them. Do not give up, though. Practice, as usual, makes perfect.

133

- If you recall having experiences like those of a psychic medium when you were a kid, chances of you rekindling those abilities in a conscious way are very high.

- Some psychic mediums will be envious of you. For that reason, you need to use your heightened senses to determine the best circle of psychics to join and which ones to avoid.

How do you change for the better once you become a psychic medium?

You are able to appreciate the eternity of life

This is because from your regular communication with spirits of the dead, you realize that life does not exactly end at death.

You cease to fear death

From your continued communication with the spirits of dead people on behalf of yourself and other people, your fear of death gets eroded. As such, you are more ready than any time ever to embrace death when your time comes.

You get to be with peace with yourself

You get this peace by nature of your role as a mediator between the living and the dead; something you cannot be effective in if your life is a mess. Besides, your spiritual guides keep communicating with you even when you are on other people's missions.

You are able to communicate with your departed

You are not just able to communicate with the spirits of your clients' departed, but also the spirits of your own family and friends.

You get to decipher some hidden truths

Sometimes people alienate themselves from others because of stereotypes or myths. However, as a psychic medium, you are able to seek guidance from your spiritual guides, thus being able to form relationships based on correct information as opposed to misguided myths.

You are able to bring peace into people's lives

By delivering people's liberating messages from their loved ones on the spiritual plane, you bring peace to their lives and help them to live meaningful lives.

You feel lucky and honored

You are also humbled by the honor others bestow on you when they entrust you with the intimate feelings between themselves and their dead loved ones. Also being able to know firsthand things that others can only know after you tell them is humbling. You, therefore, feel blessed, honored and with a great purpose in life.

Though being a psychic medium is a challenging role, it is fulfilling and honorable; and it calls on you to be all the more responsible.

Chapter 22:
How to Tell That Your 3rd Eye Is Open

Have you for a moment imagined that your two eyes might begin to pop out when your third eye opens up? That may be something some people have feared. Or possibly that a thick pimple might grow on your brow like a miner's torch... Really, none of these scary things is going to happen – not even if you turn out to be a real psychic. You will still remain the ordinary mortal you have always been. In fact, you need not fret that the pineal gland used to be on the surface at the back of your head once upon a time. That is in the history unknown to us, and it is not about to get repeated. For now, just think of that story as mythical (nice place to hide when you can't decipher things. Anyway, here is what tells you that you have your 3rd eye wide open:

Pressure within the third eye circuit

When you are not able to define it as pressure, it is possibly a tingling sensation. And sometimes that feeling is not confined to the spot between your eyebrows. You can also feel it on the crown of your head or even in other spots where different chakras are positioned. Chakras, chakras – what are they again? These are simply energy connecting points. This higher, kind of spiritual energy, is enhanced in different areas of your body depending on the role it is playing – some chakras deal with physical energy, others intuition, others self confidence, and so on. So these areas feel the impact of the enhanced flow of energy once the third eye is open. In fact, you feel the greatest sensation at the first instance when your third eye opens. Thereafter, the sensation is kind of moderate and steady.

Having a strong spiritual feeling

Here is where you feel like you are under the watch of a divine protector; a strong spiritual being; or even the spirit of a loved one. If you are religious you are likely to feel the presence of angels around you, taking care of you.

In cases where your third eye is awakened in a big way, you could even feel the presence of the loved ones of other people, not necessarily your own. And guess what that means? It means that you are progressing to the status of a medium – where you sense things on behalf of other people. That should not scare you as it is normal for heightened intuition to move in that direction.

Great desire to be a world away from negativity

When your third eye is clearly open, you find yourself being empathetic to other people. So it is inevitable for you to pick up other people's feelings. Now if those feelings happen to be negative, it leaves you drained while they themselves may appear fine and unaffected.

Owing to that sensitivity, it is understandable that you should wish to protect yourself against negativity and drama. Wholly embrace your feeling and do what you need to do – seeking to dwell in positive environments.

Great desire to maintain a healthy eating habit

Listen – different foods have got varying vibration frequencies. Did you know that? I highly doubt that you did. And why the doubt...? Well, when adjusting your diet you often cite unfavorable rounded waistline; risk of diabetes; but really nothing about vibrations. So now you know. Fruits, vegetables and such other healthy foods vibrate at higher frequencies.

And what does that mean in the whole setup of third eye opening and all?

Simple – when your third eye is open, your level of intuition is pretty high. And that directly means that you are personally vibrating at a high frequency. Is it not logical then that you should need foods that match your vibrations? In fact, and this is no exaggeration, some people take up a psychic diet. This should put any anxieties to rest – if you suddenly begin to feel inclined to walk the healthy road, it is by no means an indication that you have begun to get scared of death – no. It is a direct function of your third eye opening.

Propensity to read more

It is normal to feel like reading diverse material and synthesizing it once you have your third eye awakened. You could also find yourself leaning more towards spirituality. This follows the awareness you are having at a subconscious level on how brilliant life can be, emanating from the luminosity of your soul.

Having frequent dreams that happen to be vivid

It is not surprising that you should dream more because in your resting state that is sleep, there are no thought interruptions. So what comes in through your intuition is not inhibited by self doubt and such other forms of self conflict. Incidentally, though such dreams result from a high level of intuition, they do not necessarily translate into premonitions – so worry not that every one of your dreams will translate into reality.

Being highly sensitive to your body senses

Once you have your third eye open, your psychic senses, what you will hear being referred to as *clairs*, become stronger. Mark you here we are generally talking of the senses you already know, only in the language of psychics. In essence what you are noticing is a stronger sense of seeing; hearing; feeling; smelling; tasting; and touching; which in psychic language we call clairvoyance; clairaudience; clairsentience; clairscent; clairtangency; and clairgustance; respectively.

Having intuitive *hits*

We are talking of *hits* just to show that not everything that comes to your thoughts has a touch of reality. So these *hits* are when you are getting intuitive thoughts and they end up translating into reality. For example, you get a strong feeling about someone's presence, possibly someone who lives far away from you and someone you possibly have not seen in years and then *pap* – here they emerge! How exciting!

But then again, it may not be good things always. You may sense a bad thing and then it happens and that can be worrying. Luckily, there is a way you can retain your psychic abilities, and condition yourself to slow down on the bad things – it is called having intuitive guidance. In short, with practice, you will be able to block out the line of intuition leading to negative revelations. This way your psychic abilities will not cause you any anxiety and you can comfortably embrace them.

Experiencing frequent headaches

We are not insinuating here that every headache is a result of your high level of intuition – no. In fact many are the people with high intuition levels and yet do not suffer headaches. So seek medical assistance if the way of psychics proves ineffective.

When you think your headaches are a function of high energy influx through the sixth chakra, just soak both of your feet in some warm water. That way, you will be pulling that excess energy towards your feet and away from your head. If you wish to add some Epsom salts into the warm water, do it. If you wish to add essential oils, by all means, do it. They do a great job of relaxing your whole system.

Parting ways with some old friends and having fresh ones into your life

You see, there is nothing inherently psychic about this trend. Only that there is no way your friend is going to feel comfortable with you if she is an avid gossip and you are not into gossiping simply for its negativity. If you were materialistic earlier on and now you have relegated materialism to the back where you previously possibly put spirituality, your priorities and those of many of your old friends are bound to change. And that is alright for you will be happier with the new combination of friends; people who bring nothing but peace into your life.

Chapter 23:
The Indigo Child

No human on earth is colored Indigo, for crying out loud! Right – but being the calm person that you are, with a balanced predisposition; open to different interpretations of things and situations; you are going to see how a child can be associated with the indigo color.

Obviously, in earlier chapters here, you have seen indigo being associated with your sixth chakra or even the third eye itself. And there is even no harm in having a quick recap right here. The Root chakra goes with red; Sacral with orange; Solar Plexus with yellow; Heart with green; Throat with blue; Brow chakra with indigo; and your Crown chakra with violet. So what do you now sense is the link between the Indigo child and the third eye? Obviously, this must be a child with well developed intuition, the level that is only attained when your third eye is at its best.

Clearly that is logical. The sixth chakra is the brow chakra and it is allocated indigo as its color. And so it is understandable that a child who stands out in the abilities associated with the brow chakra be named an Indigo child. Alright! But is this color labeling solely for purposes of identification? Well, maybe and maybe not.

Were the seven chakras arbitrarily assigned their distinct colors?

Oh no! You can only hold that thought if you do not understand matters of energy flow in terms of frequency and all. But you do appreciate that angle yourself because we have even mentioned earlier on that during sessions of spiritual healing the frequency of your vibrations is at an extra high.

The point here is that there is a formula, or rather a clear basis, on which a particular chakra is associated with a particular color and not any other. And it goes like this:

There is light traveling from Point A to Point B within space, and you can call that distance *wavelength*. That distance of a single wave is measured in nanometers (nm) and wavelengths on average range from 380 to 740 nanometers. Waves have vibrations along the way and those can have a relatively low or relatively high frequency. Now, to reflect a particular color, there is a specific combination of factors – the number of waves moving together; their vibrations; and even the frequency of those vibrations. What that combination essentially gives you is energy. And that energy comes in a Sine wave. So you have light waves that are in waveform, moving and vibrating at very high frequency to form a Sine wave.

The totality of those factors visually comes as color; each color depending on the wavelength in nanometers as well as frequency in Terahertz (THz). A Terahertz is actually a unit measure of electromagnetic frequency equivalent to a trillion hertz. And remember the Sine wave is a measure of that energy that you now see in color. And that energy is what you have traveling through your chakras and relating with energies outside of your body as well.

Here are the wavelength as well as frequency ranges for the chakra colors:

	Red	Orange	Yellow	Green	Blue	Indigo	Violet
Wavelength (nm)	625 - 740	590 - 625	565 - 590	520 – 565	500 - 520	435 - 500	380 - 435
Frequency (THz)	400 - 484	484 - 508	508 - 526	526 – 606	606 - 670	670 - 700	700 - 789

Do you remember chakras to be energy fields? If you do, then you know that there must be vibrations and frequencies there too. So, understandably, the wavelengths within you and those that come in form of external light have a way of matching so that those compatible work together. And that can tell you outright that the frequency of vibrations at your brow chakra must be in the range of 670 to 700 THz – the range of frequency that creates the aura color, Indigo.

You need to realize that each color is only a physical manifestation of the light spectrum that you have within a given frequency range. None of those colors that incidentally happen to be the colors of the rainbow is of greater importance than any other. They only help you to know how to work with your chakras to improve your health and general wellbeing.

Abilities of the Indigo Child

Basically, the reason a child qualifies to get the reference Indigo child is the manifestation of heightened intuition and significantly high intelligence. Such a child often displays exemplary genius and abilities of telekinetic or psychic nature. Generally, their overall abilities – biological; mental; and also spiritual happen to be more advanced than the average kid.

The kid also has high self esteem while showing signs of admirable integrity.

Be warned:

An Indigo child can read manipulation for what it is despite being young in age. They can easily detect when you have a hidden agenda and will not fall for it. Amazingly, young as they may be, Indigo children are averse to pettiness. They prefer to work independently, not because they dislike other people, but because they would rather they came up with their own solutions – they are that confident about their abilities. Besides, they revel in being able to search, in their belief that it is possible to get solutions to issues.

That trait often gets them identified as non-conformists. And it is really an actual truth because if you think about it, Indigo children do not like being restricted within rigid structures. In any case, who with all the heightened awareness and intellect would wish to be boxed in an environment of mundane rules of dos and don'ts? They would feel gagged and under-utilized, a state that can even harm their well being. That is why they usually appear explosive under such restricting environments, as they seek to do things their way, even exploring where the powers that be have not given them authority to dig.

Can You Convert An Indigo Child?

In fact, that nature of Indigo children is not something they can turn on and off at will – it is natural. As scientists struggle to agree or disagree on the issue of whether really 96% of your DNA is utterly useless or not, it is believed that the DNA of Indigo children is all useful. And that is the reason they can comprehend things that ordinary children their age will not at all levels – physical; mental; as well as spiritual. Of course, they also have abilities that the average adult does not have as well and that is because of those spiritual healing abilities that innately exist in them.

So, no; you cannot convert an Indigo child from the highly imaginative, intuitive and sensitive child that they are, to just an average kid. It would be frustrating for both of you to try and do so, and in any case, there is no need for it.

Chapter 24:
How to identify and Make use of Aura Colors

Did you know you could capture your aura color photographically? After so much debate and skepticism about the existence of aura colors, a guy by the name of Guy Coggins finally designed an aura camera that could capture your distinct aura. That was back in the '70s. Before that, the talk of aura colors could only be confidently discussed with psychics and mediums, people who could appreciate spiritual visualization of things otherwise not visible to the naked eye.

Of course, today things are somewhat different. For example, you have read that aura colors are not arbitrarily given to individuals but rather each color is determined by the intensity, speed and frequency of the energy wavelengths. And knowing that the way a camera captures photographs has a lot to do with intensity of light and speed, you can see how plausible it is to assert that a camera has the capacity to capture aura colors.

How to Identify Auras Using Your Ordinary Standard Camera

With science at work, you do not need to use a specialized aura camera to capture someone's aura color. However, there are a few tips that will help you do it better:

Be close to your subject

For you to capture the aura decisively using a conventional camera, you need to be in close proximity to your subject. And yes, most modern cameras have the zoom facility, but that is not the one to help you this time. You need to be physically close.

146

Your subject needs to have a strong aura

Unless you want to do trial and error forever, you need to use a subject in the category that has obvious strong auras.

- A psychic or a medium, for example, should have a strong aura that will be captured clearly and distinctly on camera. This is because these are people whose chakras are well open and they have their spiritual energies flowing in a clear uninhibited manner.

- In fact, any spiritual person would make for a good subject. Spiritual people, whatever faith they follow, usually have high spiritual consciousness, and that makes for strong auras.

- Any person with their third eye open can make great subjects for aura photography. This is because having the third eye open is indication that spiritual energies that will be the target of the camera are strong.

- A child can make a good subject for aura photography. Innocent as they are, they have barely anything that might inhibit the great natural flow of spiritual energy. As such, their aura colors are bound to show clearly and distinctly.

Make your place of photography clutter free

You know how clutter even in your own house can adversely affect your emotions. Now, when seeking to identify your aura color, you want it natural and not when adulterated or blurred by an instant mood change brought about by a cluttered environment.

So it is advisable that your venue of aura photography be clear and welcoming. And the background needs to be one of solid colors. Many experts suggest you give your background plain neutral colors, say like black; deep blue; or even white that can do some good reflection. The idea here is to get your subject well illuminated.

And if you have a child as your subject, it would help to let the child have something nice, say a toy or a pet such as a kitten. When the child is happy, its aura color is bound to show more distinctly.

Use lighting to illuminate your subject

In order to capture someone well in a photograph, it is important that the person be well illuminated. That illumination is also necessary in capturing the person's aura color as well. In this kind of photography, you cannot trust your camera flash the way you do when taking photographs in poorly lit areas. Instead, it is advisable to place lamps and possibly photo lights in strategic locations that will ensure that your subject is properly illuminated.

How does it help to know people's aura colors?

First of all, the reason you want your third eye open is to be able to understand yourself and other people beyond what you see physically. In understanding the way people behave emotionally and spiritually, you can relate with them better and also live in harmony with them. In the process, the earthly person that you are, you get to know how to handle each individual in the best way possible, so that you can easily get your agendas through at work and in business; you keep off antagonism when danger looms; and you are generally happy.

Now, these are the same principles on which the importance of aura colors lie. Knowing whether a person is a blue, red or whatever other color prepares you to relate with them cohesively, and it makes you better placed to help them when nobody else seems to appreciate their feelings.

Colors and Matching Characteristics

Have we said that a person's aura color is an indication of what kind of person he or she is? That is correct. And the kind of person one is happens to be in terms of likes and dislikes; and also temperament.

Red

People whose aura color is red like challenges. And they work hard. In addition, they express their will strongly. So, they are those kinds of people that you will usually find in leadership and in sports. They are also courageous and adventurous and have high survival instincts. In fact, you should not be surprised to capture red in most of the children you photograph, and especially the male kids.

But beware of cloudy red: If the shade you are seeing is a cloudy red, this person has intense negative energy, possibly from deep rooted anger. Have you heard people say they hate so and so with a passion? These are the people likely to fall into this category.

Orange

These ones love adventure too and are courageous and independent; but they also happen to be well organized. They happen to be ambitious, confident and intuitive; and they have originality and ability to express themselves well. They are also pretty open and sociable.

Yellow

People with Yellow as their aura color have high intellect and are spontaneous. They are usually happy and pretty optimistic; and they have the tendency to illuminate their surrounding bringing warmth to the people around. They may appear playful, alright, but they are good at picking the details in any interaction. Above all, they are highly disciplined.

Green

Greens hold themselves in high esteem and are goal focused. They are usually go-getters who want to be in control of things. They pursue their goals tenaciously. However, they are caring too and enjoy teaching.

You will usually find people with green as their aura color running their own businesses; involved in matters of spiritual healing; teaching or even in the medical profession.

But ever heard the saying green with envy? Well, dark or cloudy green is what comes out as the aura color when the person is overwhelmed with jealousy as well as resentment. And they will not even own up responsibility for their bad deeds.

Blue

Blues speak and act with wisdom. They are reliable; the kind whose word you can take to the bank. They are loyal, honest and generous; and they are sensitive and peace loving. They are empathetic and have a warm heart. Often, you find them spiritual. And they happen to be good listeners though you cannot also help but like the way they talk.

But as for dark blue, there is trouble in paradise. This person does not trust what the future holds yet facing the truth is a challenge because the person wants to remain in full control.

Indigo

If you are thinking compassion and gentleness, the Indigos are it. They are the tolerant and charitable lot that you usually find in humanitarian missions. They are observant and liberal, and they are open-minded too. They are also intuitive, perceptive and also shrewd.

Violet

If you have ever thought of people to label daydreamers, Violets fit that. Whereas they are intuitive and spiritual, they also tend in live in a world of fantasy. They attain what they want without seeming to push too hard. They are an unconventional lot that seems to seek magical solutions to issues. They are usually spiritual and also mystical.

Question: Are those seven colors all that you see of coloration around you?

Of course not! The world is full of colors you may not care to count. And that is because most are either shades of those seven colors of the rainbow, or they are a direct mix of some of those colors.

In terms of auras, then, it is safe to say that you are not always going to reflect your basic color like red or green. And the reason is that there is a lot happening around you at any one time that affects your aura. If you recall, even non-living things have some of that aura – the fact that they have energy in them backs that up. Think of crystals and the light that moves within them to produce shades of color. The energies from people and things around you have a way of meeting with your own energies either making yours stronger or destabilizing it.

Here are other colors that come up in auras

White

People with the white aura are kind of survivors; chameleon-like. They kind of assimilate colors from others around them, and the intention is to remain protected. They are people of great wisdom, capable of seeing the bigger picture. They are bright; avid readers who also love theater, movies and television particularly as a source of social information; and they happen to be highly motivated.

White can also denote the person's high level of spirituality; associating the color with newness or purity just the way it was depicted in ancient times when angelic beings were seen surrounded by white auras.

Magenta

While magentas are creative, imaginative, innovative and inventive, they are also good at manipulating other people. They are non-conformists whose mind is a kind of restless. You can also aptly describe them as being strong willed and resourceful.

Aqua

People whose aura is aqua have a longing to be recognized. They are sensitive and prone to stress and anxiety. If your image has aqua on the portion above the position of your head, it means that music is very important in your life.

Pink

People with the pink aura love art as well as beauty in general. They are well intentioned people with a great sense in matters of companionship. Pinks are also loving. And if you are taking a photograph of a person who has fallen head over heels for someone, you are likely to capture a good deal of that pink aura.

How about dark pink? Ah-ah... That is bad news. Such a person is deceitful; dishonest; and manifests immaturity.

Gray

The gray aura is indication that some chakras are blocked; and you are not able to trust any person or even anything.

Black

The black aura indicates a person in deep focus but not towards any good. Here is a person who has done well in absorbing all other auras from the environment so that no good seems to prevail. The spirit hovering around is about lack of forgiveness and other negative feelings.

Alternatively, there are negative energies that have converged somewhere in the body and are causing disease.

Chapter 25:
How to Be Supportive to Your Indigo Child

Is it possible to tell, for instance, that your child has potential to become a great athlete; a great singer; a leader; or something like that? It, definitely, is possible. The little things that your child says or does; and even the manner of doing it; your child's demeanor; all these can be pointers to what direction your kid is set to follow later in life. Of course, there is a lot of potential lost along the way, courtesy of the ignorance of adults in the kid's life, parents included; and other environmental factors. But suppose each child were to grow into an adult utilizing his or her full potential! Oh my! Lots of problems you see today would never exist. And that includes poverty and wars.

Now, the reason you are able to become a supportive parent rather than a hindrance is because you can presumably identify your child's potential in whatever it is. In this particular case, you can only be of assistance to your Indigo child if you have noticed and acknowledged that the child falls under this category of Indigo children who also go by the reference Crystal children.

Now, you may be aware, especially after reading informative material as what you find in this book, that Indigo children are highly intelligent; highly stimulated and motivated; highly imaginative; and with great memory. But since having such a talented child is not necessarily something you may have anticipated, it is possible to miss or downplay the signs. Worst of all, you may try to suppress them. To avert such unfortunate responses towards the Indigo children, it is advisable for parents to pay attention to their kids' development on the premise that each child is unique.

And what can you say about yourself? If you were to be asked, would you say you are in that category of Indigo or Crystal Children? You know if you can answer that either in the affirmative or in the negative, you can determine how to handle yourself and your abilities amidst other people who are like you and those unlike you. And with that awareness you get to avoid disappointments and frustrations. With the right information, you will not succumb to the uncomfortable feeling arising from being tagged ill through modern conventional ways of gauging character and behavior. In fact, you can easily ignore the common label often given to extra active and imaginative kids –Attention Deficit Disorder or Attention Deficit Hyperactivity Disorder (ADD or ADHD).

Here Are Questions That Should Attract A *Yes* When You Are Indigo:

- Do you feel like you could achieve more than the world allows you to? In other words, are you always searching for something more meaningful in life and which does not seem available for people of your ilk?

- Do you feel too wise for your chronological age?

- Do you encounter difficulties trying to fit into conventional society owing to the way people operate?

- Do you often feel like fish out of water just being around other people?

- Do you find yourself standing alone on many issues due to your divergent perception of the world?

- Do you find your intuition much stronger than that of most other people?

- Do you find people misunderstanding you when you speak naturally to them?

- Do you sense this overwhelming feeling that you are on a mission in this world – like there is a special purpose you were born?

- Do you feel like your beliefs radically differ from those of other people?

- Do you feel like everyone takes you to be your family's black sheep? In fact, do you feel that your family hardly understands you?

- Do you feel ill at ease until you find people who see things like you do?

- Do you consider yourself highly sensitive emotionally?

- Did you encounter a trying childhood?

- Are you uncomfortable with too much authority around you; authority that makes you have the feeling of being disempowered?

And just in case you feel like the affirmative answers to those questions are not conclusive, you may wish to consult a clairvoyant. What the clairvoyant is going to do then is level with your energy, detecting the frequency of the vibrations around you – your aura – and if that energy that is, obviously, invisible turns out to be Indigo, that is clear affirmation for you.

Importance of knowing if you are indigo or not

First of all, after knowing that you are indigo, you will know when to get involved in a debate and when to become a spectator. If you can tell that none of the participants can see at your level, you might as well avoid upsetting situations. And in situations where the society has given up on someone, you may just be the right person to help out. No wonder as an Indigo child you feel like an individual on a mission. You will enjoy your life better when you appreciate yourself as an Indigo child, and as a parent you will help your Indigo child better in many ways, but the most apt is making the environment conducive; meaning harmonious as opposed to destabilizing.

Chapter 26:
How to Bring Much Needed Harmony into Your Home

What is this harmony? Obviously, it is not like talking of bringing riches home because with riches you are just looking at the money and basically what money can buy. But harmony is even more valuable because it makes you enjoy your wealth, relationships and everything else better than if it did not exist.

Call it oneness and integration – an environment where you do not change and your child does not change in terms of likes and dislikes; but you find yourselves co-existing and being supportive of one another. In such an environment, your energies continue to flow in a healthy way, and whoever has a high intuition continues on spiritual journeys uninhibited. In short, when there is harmony in the home or even at your workplace, every person enjoys goodwill from all around and there is mutual contentment. At the end of the day, every person is able to reach their potential and achieve their goals. Of course, everyone dreads what happens in the absence of harmony which happens to be frustration; annoyance; unutilized talent and unfulfilled goals.

How Do You Achieve Harmony?

Taking deep breaths

When your Indigo child appears rowdy in that hyperactive mode, ask them to halt, take in deep breaths through the nose, and subsequently release that volume of air out through the mouth. It is helpful when the exhalation is decisive and not just a by-the-way because it comes out with excessive emotions in the kid. If the kid was in anger, it will be a way of calming him or her down. This is something you can get yourself to do too if you are Indigo, but when it comes to your kid, you need to make it fun. In fact, whether you are Indigo yourself or not, you can choose to do this inhaling and exhaling thing with your kid just to help the kid embrace it.

Smudging

You need to get into the habit of smudging your house so as to reinstate the harmony that normally exists. Sometimes when your kids and other family members venture out in public, they return home having their individual energies destabilized and it does not do any good to any of you, particularly your Indigo child.

And just in case you are not in the loop, this is not the smudging where you mar your walls with paint or soot – no. This smudging is some form of spiritual cleansing that sweeps away all the negative energy within the vicinity. In fact, it comes in handy like when you have had hot arguments, reason being that you want everyone in the house to remain emotionally healthy whether you have resolved your bone of contention or not. This is something helpful especially when you, your child or any other member of your family is Indigo; in which case, this book will guide you on how to smudge.

Seeking to stay grounded

Here you invoke spiritual power by doing some visualizing exercise. You focus on your root chakra, which obviously, is the one in charge of your grounding, and you let a clear cord emerge from the spot of your tail bone, dangling down towards the ground. Essentially what you are trying to do here is give all the negative energy within you an outlet. So spiritually, you ask Mother Earth to accept that cord from your body, and as you do that you ensure you exhale meaningfully.

Mother Earth is full of healthy life giving energy. So your exercise will not be complete without you asking for a good dose of that. Therefore once you feel satisfied that your negative energy has exited your body and been swallowed by the earth, you embark on inhaling Mother Earth's positive energy – with deep intent. Now thank Mother Earth for her support and generosity and enjoy your fresh harmony. You will often hear the word *Gaia* being mentioned in this context and that is because that is what the Greeks used to call their goddess of the Earth.

Use a shield

Every fighter carries a shield of sorts, and even in specialties like karate you learn how to do a shielding move. When you are as sensitive as the way an Indigo child is, you are in constant threat from negative forces in terms of negative emotions from depressed people; angry people; hateful ones; vengeful ones; and such other people who just speak of doom and failure. If you are not well shielded, you stand to absorb those negative emotions like a sponge absorbing liquids – and that is worse for you than an average person who does not care what happens to other people in the world.

The way you create your shield is by spiritually visualizing a strong bubble of white light surrounding you each morning. That works by having positive energies in the environment matching the vibrations of your own positive energy and therefore they merge and you become even more emotionally stronger. Then as protection, your protective ring of white light repels all the negative energies being discharged by other forces.

Exercising

Exercising is not just great because it helps you trim down excess fat – no. It trims down negative emotions too. And especially because Indigo kids have their nervous systems wired entirely different from the average person, they get to be affected more by what is happening around them. The good thing is that any physical exercise will help release the negative emotions being bottled up whether emotionally; mentally; physically; or even spiritually. Many psychics, of course, like going for the martial arts; karate; tai chi; and dance classes, but there is a good number who also go for gymnastics; running; and even skipping.

Let your home reflect nature

Oh, how peaceful it feels to sit in a place surrounded by trees and other vegetation; watching some soothing waterfall and some calming crystals; or even admiring fish moving about in an aquarium...

Having some quiet space

You need to have a place where someone can just sit in peace and quiet – a place where you can meditate if you want to; draw things from your imagination; let your mind play by doing word and other puzzles; read; do anything that just makes you feel good and relaxed.

Bathing in sea salt

Having night baths where you put some sea salt in your bath water is a good way of expelling toxins from your physical body. The salty water also works at your energies, pulling out the negative ones and leaving you feeling relaxed in a pretty balanced way.

Using sea salt on the names

You could have the name of your Indigo child written somewhere and then sprinkle sea salt on it. If you give it a day as it is, say 24hrs, the salt will have had the impact of pulling out the negative energies within your child; and you can then wipe off the salt and dump it in the toilet.

Getting rid of artificial scents

It is advisable to avoid using cheap perfumes within your environment. You would rather burn beeswax candles that are not scented. But if you prefer some scent around you, you need to go for the high quality stuff, including oils.

Play energy friendly music

Energy friendly...? Yes – music that does not disturb your energy flow; not the kind of loud music with chaotic vibrations. The type that works well to stabilize your energy fields is angelic music; classical; melodic; and such calming tunes.

Clear the bedroom of electrical gadgets

Things like television and computers in the bedroom have the negative effect of destabilizing the energy fields with their electromagnetic waves. So when you clear your bedroom of such electrical equipment, there is harmony that lets you enjoy deep, peaceful sleep.

Avoid manipulation

Indigo children are averse to manipulation. If you have psychic abilities, you will understand that quite well. So to create a harmonious environment for your child, you need to level with him or her at all times.

Chapter 27:
What, exactly, is Smudging?

What, for the love of harmony in the home, is smudging? The previous chapter speaks of smudging the house after you and your folks have been out. It also suggests that smudging is helpful after you have had a scuffle; a hot disagreement; or such other emotional confrontation in your home.

What, then, is smudging?

As already mentioned, smudging in this context has nothing to do with adding more mess by dropping dots of paint or marring walls with soot. It actually carries the opposite connotation – of cleansing. And if you want to know where the smudging act was borrowed from, well, it is a Native American tradition.

The natives would cleanse themselves and the environment by using smudging, by then commonly known as Sacred Smoke Bowl Blessing. This custom that usually preceded traditional ceremonies was some form of psychic cleansing. In fact, you can equate that to the way you wash your hands before doing something sensitive such as putting food into your mouth. With the Native Americans, they would burn sage or such other herbs that were deemed sacred, and the spirits of those plants would bring back their peace and balance.

In fact, if you check further into history, you will appreciate that different cultures had their unique ways of cleansing and blessing, most of which involved burning some natural items. You will find them among the ancient Maori of New Zealand; Zulus of South Africa; Balinese of Indonesia; and others. And you can even come more modern and see how the church, usually the Catholic, cleanses its inside by burning incense.

And do not imagine that ancient church gong, or strong bell, was just signal time for mass. It also had presumably the role of cleansing the parish through its sound and in the process influencing the community around into moving to the church.

Anyway, today, there is a scientific angle to the whole business of smudging because evidently, burning sage and similar herbs releases negative ions. And there has been strong linkage of these ions to the positive mood you end up developing. The presumption is that everything around you has energies, some of them with the possibility of being negative. In fact, things around you absorb the negative energies that you release when you quarrel and do disruptive things. And so by smudging, you manage to get rid of any negative energies that those things in the vicinity may be harboring and which they may be releasing into the environment. Those are energies that have the potential of making their way into you and so you need to be protected – fending off all emotional as well as psychic garbage.

How Burning Of Sage Helps In Smudging

Is the aroma great? Surely, it is. And as you enjoy it your brain is also receiving a bigger supply of oxygen, thanks to the sage burning. As a result, your muscles relax and you become less tense. And is the smoke any good? Well, better than you would imagine – altering the molecular structure of the air around you and also positively affecting the energy around you to produce great cleansing effect on the overall. The smell itself works on your instincts and memory, making for amazing aromatherapy. The whole process has the welcome effect of combating fear; grief; resentment; frustrations; anger; and even depression.

Useful Items For Smudging

Smudging, like most things that you do to enhance your third eye, is well thought out. Every process is linked to the flow of your spiritual energy. In the case of smudging, you want to connect with the nature and so you have four basic elements of nature symbolically represented. You have got fire; you have water; you have air; and then there is the earth itself. Here is how they are symbolized:

- Fire: this is symbolized by burning herbs

- Water: this is symbolized by a shell, and often it is an abalone shell

- Air: this is symbolized by the smoke

- Earth: this one is symbolized by the unlit herbs

Sometimes you find something added to the mix to symbolize the spirit.

Herbs Used In Smudging

As for the choice of herbs, sage is the most preferred. It has varieties and the most commonly used happens to be the desert sage. This is still the one they refer to as sand sage or even Rose sage. Its fragrance is amazing and its burning instantly lifts your spirits.

There are times sage gets mixed with sweet grass to make smudge sticks. In such cases, the sticks burn and the sage in them deals with the negative energies around while the sweet grass plays the role of attracting any reachable positive energies.

You can use other herbs effectively in smudging as often happens including:

- Cedar

- Juniper

- Lavender

Of course, this list is not exhaustive. For instance, the Incas of Ecuador go for the San Palo wood right in the rainforest, which they consider Holy Wood, and they use it in smudging. And do not be surprised to see some Indian tribe using tobacco for this very purpose of smudging.

Distinct Properties of Different Herbs

Sage

This one is brings calm and healing; and also enhances your wisdom

Lavender

This one attracts the energies and spirits that embrace loving. It also has a tendency to restore balance creating an all-peaceful atmosphere.

Sweet grass

As already mentioned, this one has a way of attracting positive energy

Cedar

This one is used with different agendas in mind, among those being the obvious one of smudging. It wipes off negative energies within the area and also draws the positive energy. In the ritual of blessing a home, cedar comes in handy too. In fact, in a nutshell, cedar may just be the herb you want for heightened spiritual awareness. It is associated with enhanced clairvoyance and restoration of an exhausted mind and a tired body; as well as stimulation of your spirit.

Mugwort

One of the precious things the Mugwort does is banishing spirits of evil nature. Above that it stimulates your intuition and imagination; and the result is heightened psychic awareness as well as clearer prophetic dreams.

Juniper

This one is purely for spiritual purification. In its cleansing, it creates for you a sacred place that is entirely safe to dwell in.

Yerba Santa

This one is burnt for the purpose of purification, and it also sets boundaries within which you can dwell in full protection.

Rosemary

This one is great for enhancing your ability to appreciate issues with clarity.

Is there a quick fix when you cannot do conventional smudging?

Well, understandably, you could enter a room and feel overwhelmed by the thickness of negative energy and you know that such a situation does not augur well for your spiritual energy. Gladly, there is something you can do to feel better and safer and that is smearing yourself with some variety of essential oil made from sage. Palo Santo oil would also do. And even a spray form of those sage and Palo Santo products in the room would help kick out the negative energy.

Alternatively, you can do something entirely spiritual – no physical items but just you and your spiritual connection. Here, you calmly but intensely visualize the room filled with light that is a clear white. Then you begin to push out the light, and as it moves, it is pushing out the negative energies that initially made the atmosphere in the room heavy. At the end of that exercise, you will remain with a clear room that feels great to be in.

Suppose you cannot do burning and you know nil about using light?

You still can use your chosen herbs even when it is prohibited or not convenient to burn things where you are. Here are helpful tips:

- You could steep your chosen herbs in essential oil or even in water

What happens when you do that is creation of a tincture that you can then sprinkle in your space of concern or even spray the zone with it.

- Place salt next to a window

Often, people opt for Himalayan salt and it works well. What you do is place it near your window, possibly on the window sill, and then after sometime you come back and dispose of that salt preferably right in the ground. The process of cleansing takes place here by having the salt absorb all the negative energies within the place, and thereafter disposing them in the ground from where they cannot return.

Chapter 28:
How You Can Close Your Third Eye

For starters, why would you wish to close your powerful third eye? Well, there may be varying reasons for this. If you have been on the farm, for example, and observed a farmer opening a goat pen, you may have seen how young rams behave once the pen is open: they ran amok! The farmer may smile about that but it would be a different ball game if the rams continued that behavior for hours on end. The farmer may have to call a veterinary doctor to check the animals with a view to taming them.

This is the same case that happens sometimes. You may open your third eye and begin experiencing the power of vision that comes with it; the swirling energy on your brow; intuition that proves 100% reality; and vivid reading of your environment. While this can be exciting, supposing you continued to visualize every potential happening on a continuous basis? Would it not overwhelm you after a while? In fact, chances are that you may find yourself being privy to occurrences you would rather you did not know – and that can be unsettling. At this juncture, if you had your way, you would close that third eye in an instant.

Other times you may just want to temper that psychic power of awareness just a little bit. Here is one way you can turn off your third eye or tone down your intuition:

Deliberately switching focus from your third eye. There are many ways to do that. Here are some you could try:

- Tell yourself that you seriously want to get out of that spiritual energy and return to your normal surroundings. By suggesting you tell yourself, the meaning is that you deliberately try to focus your energy away from your 6th chakra and possibly onto other chakras that deal with the physique.

- Switch your focus on your physical surrounding, or even on doing mundane stuff.

- You could do something which can contribute to stimulating your root chakra, hence making you grounded in your actions and relationships too. Examples of activities you can engage in for that purpose include clearing your house of clutter and keeping yourself busy organizing it.

- Pay attention to details of your daily life, including analyzing your bills and paying them; analyzing your bank account and possibly doing some bank reconciliations; such things that distract you from psychic energy.

- Engage in some physical exercises like jogging; table tennis; or just walking.

- Getting a massage.

Disconnecting from the realm of the psychic

It is not automatic that you get yourself from matters of the head in a moment especially once you have been in it for some time, but it is important that you work on it. If you allow yourself to remain in that state of heighted intuition, you may get a shock when something happens in your immediate surroundings abruptly. So you need to make a deliberate effort to retain reasonable awareness of your worldly environment even as you get your third eye energies flowing.

Involve yourself in mundane stuff and routine

You could, for instance, get into the routine of taking breakfast; reading the dailies; watching mainstream media; and not doing anything creative at all. With time you will see no visions and you will stop sensing anything intuitive. This is because while you were busy attending to mundane stuff, visions surfaced but you did not pay attention to them and so they left. Soon, your third eye closes.

Well, this is not Greek or Latin: just simple English. And you will appreciate this when you consider how much people talk around you and you do not register a thing. Why? This is simply because you have deliberately kept your focus elsewhere – maybe an e-mail you were replying to; a bank statement you were analyzing; and so on.

Discard your own belief that the third eye exists

How is that possible? Well, just like athletes on the track, if you begin second guessing yourself, you will slow down. The reason you succeed is because you remain focused. So when you want to close your third eye, telling your mind that the whole belief system was a joke and that the whole psychic business is not possible begins to weaken your psychic abilities.

If you find it difficult to convince yourself since you believe in the third eye anyway, try discussing the topic with skeptics. They will emphasize to you how crazy it is for anyone to believe in such power of intuition, and that will begin to make dents on your belief too. If you keep at it, soon you will have your psychic awareness dropping, and in due course your third eye will close.

Important Facts Concerning the Third Eye

We are happy when our third eye is open especially because we feel confident we know where we are in life. But as observed above, if uncontrolled, your psychic awareness can overwhelm you to the extent you want it off. However, there are times when you want to enhance your psychic awareness and have your third eye clear, yet you do not reach your optimum. You need to be aware of the things that you can do and end up sabotaging your personal efforts – like:

Staying up late and sleeping irregular times

How is that negative in strengthening the vision of the third eye? Well, the way the pineal gland works has a connection with the 24hr cycle of the earth's rotations. So, for your third eye to function optimally, you need to adhere to the natural day's cycle. You use natural light working in the daytime, and you use artificial light minimally before you go to bed.

Intense use of technology

You are bound to find it difficult retaining your psychic awareness if you are spending hours and hours on your laptop, your iphone and so on. These gadgets have artificial light that travels at unimaginable speed, and that, inevitably, affects your pineal gland. In fact, word has it that this techno-culture has weakened the genetic ability you used to have to ward off nightmares.

Chapter 29:
Interesting Facts Regarding the Third Eye

Did you know that you and everyone else you know have psychic powers? Well, that is the fact, only that just as there is latent and kinetic energy, some people have active psychic powers while others have theirs dormant. Meaning...? What that actually means is that you may have intuition about something and acknowledge it, yet others never give room for possibilities of intuition; they block the idea out and always wait to see logic before accepting there may be a chance of unsubstantiated occurrences.

If you want to tell if you are one of the people who acknowledge and appreciate intuition, people whose 3rd eye is open, there are certain things you can observe.

Here – How To Tell You Have Natural Psychic Abilities

Seek to answer the questions below, and if some of your answers are in the affirmative, then you know your 3rd eye is open – you have a high intuition level:

- Do you find yourself thinking of somebody and almost immediately your phone rings and it is them on the line; or better still, they appear from nowhere?

- Do you sometimes have a hunch about something and when you ignore it you come to regret having done so?

- Are you able to tell from the onset if you like or dislike someone when you meet them for the first time?

- Are you sometimes certain about the outcome of an event even before it takes place?

- Do you sometimes guess a person's profession, without the benefit of hearing them speak and without being guided by the manner of dressing, and you are spot on?

- Do you experience vivid dreams of a prophetic nature?

- Do you get many coincidences and synchronicities in your life?

Some of us do have these signs of great intuition, but we push them into the background because we are scared of what seems mysterious and strange. But you need not do that. Granted, it is normal to try and protect yourself from what you may fear to be harmful – like trying to bar anything that may seem to make you feel a little crazy – but the downside is that right there you could be blocking out some very nice things that could bring optimism and hope to your life. You could even miss a lifetime friend just because you thought your strong intuition about them was strange.

There Is Nothing Crazy About Having Psychic Abilities

Be happy you can tap into your intuitive abilities. Everyone else has this intricate inner guidance system, but not everyone is able to benefit from it. There is actually nothing magical about the whole thing and it is not something you can associate with any religious faith – it is simply human. Human beings are themselves a great force of energy. Everything else around us has some energy too. Is it strange then that you should be able to have some unspoken communication with fellow human beings and with all things on earth?

If you follow that simple logic, you will realize that surely there is nothing really incomprehensible about having psychic abilities. In fact, the reason we often miss it is the preoccupation we have with conventions of society and other conditions that get the sensitivity of the third eye suppressed.

Some people have distinct psychic abilities

We have been speaking of you thinking of something and it happens; you having a good feeling about someone and you end up getting a lifetime connection with them; things that affect you. But guess what? You could go a notch higher and be able to tell things that affect other people – like the example of guessing someone's profession and it turns out right; or even being able to tell them what they are going to become later in life. That is being psychic. It means that other people can rely on you to warn them against impending danger and you end up protecting them; or they could rely on you to pick the right option when it comes to life choices.

Psychics may have varying fields of strength

Just like in school where we say that so and so is bright but is a math genius or a science guru, it is the same with psychics. Some have incredibly strong intuition relating to sight; others relating to the sense of touch; others relating to the sense of hearing; and so on. In that regard, we have psychics that can be categorized as:

- Clairvoyants

- Clairaudients

- Clairsensitives

- Remote viewers

- Lucid projectors

- Lucid dreamers

- Precognitors

- Retrocognitors

- Telepaths

In reality, psychics have the ability to strengthen even those intuitive abilities they were initially not so strong in. This is because they are already good at making good use of those high level energies. It then means that you could find a person who accurately hears sounds of happenings far off – the Clairaudient – being able to tie those sounds to actual events happening in real time, and even seeing the actual people involved in those events – meaning you are a remote viewer too.

Alright! That is getting a little deep now – but clearly understandable. We all have our third eye, but only part of us behave in ways that encourage it to open and add awareness to the sensitivity of our five common senses. You see with your naked eyes; feel with your physical body; hear with your ears; taste with your tongue; and smell with your nose. But guess what – even if you lost those senses but had your third eye well open, you could still make sense of what is happening around you and know what kind of people exist in this wide world. Oh... Is that the same as being a medium?

Well, not necessarily.

So, what is a medium?

For one, you are right to the extent that a medium is a psychic. But you cannot flip that conversely – a psychic is not necessarily a medium. You see, a medium can communicate with the spiritual world – yes, even the spirits themselves! But you as a psychic can only communicate with me and others, and also things, through the link in energies.

Simply put, what you as a psychic have in common with a medium is the ability to see someone's past life; the current life; and also the future trend. However, when you have the abilities of a medium, you find yourself getting assistance of knowing things from the spirits of people departed and other divine powers. That is why you can see a medium telling you how your late grandpa looked like and the kind of voice he had; whether he is happy with what you are doing now or not; and possibly what you should do to remedy an unpleasant situation you may be in.

Can you learn to be a medium?

Seriously, very few things are impossible with the help of the spiritual powers. We have already seen that you are capable of developing your psychic abilities even when all along you had your third eye closed. With the art of becoming a medium, you just need the right teacher plus the right level of patience to take you through the necessary practice. But we must acknowledge that being a medium is a pretty rare gift.

How To Know You Are A Natural Medium

First and foremost, if you are a natural, the things you experience do not begin after an incident or an accident. They also do not begin to happen after you undergo some seminar or such other training. You do not also begin to experience them at maturity. You begin to experience extraordinary things without any prompting or any jerking from a traumatic experience; and also without any training towards that end.

Here are some telltale signs that you are a born natural when it comes to the exceptional abilities of a medium:

- You can feel the physical presence of someone invisible in the room, something that others with you cannot detect. In similar circumstances, you may feel a cold breeze yet you know there is no wind sweeping through.

- You could find yourself sometimes hearing voices even when nobody is physically speaking around you. You may clearly hear people whispering or even hear your name being called out as if someone wants your attention.

- You may find yourself receiving messages in your dreams, possibly from departed relatives or friends. And it is not always that the messages are meant for you; sometimes they are meant for other people. That is how you get to mediate, as a medium, between the living and the dead.

- Sometimes you get communication from a super power, a spiritual power, giving you insights into things you otherwise would not have known. This may come in form of a conversation within you – a kind of debate – that leaves you with a clear perspective.

- It becomes common for you to see apparitions from the very corners of your eyes.

Chapter 30:
The Cohesive Relationship Amongst The 1st, 2nd And 3rd Eye

Really – there is a first eye? And there is a second one? And these are not in reference to the pair you have on your face? That is interesting! But logical, though. You cannot be talking of the 3rd eye unless you are acknowledging the existence of a first and a second eye.

So which are these two preceding eyes?

First of all, you have got your physical sight. Call that your 1st eye. It is your visual sense. Then you have got your sense of reasoning; and reflection too. That now is your 2nd eye. These two eyes work pretty well together as you can detect from the common saying:

'If it looks like a duck, swims like a duck, and quacks like a duck, then it probably is a duck'.

So your sight tells you how the animal looks like and how it walks. Then your reasoning tells you that if you add the familiar sound of quacking, then it is unlikely to be anything else but the bird that does all those things – the duck.

The 3rd eye completing your mental picture

Even where your sight brought about a maybe; and your reasoning added the intensity of the possibility; the strength of your third eye comes in to clear any doubts and indicates: yes, it is; or no, it isn't. So these three senses work in- tandem with one another to tell you how things are for real.

In essence, it is like speaking of a trinity of sorts – your body, your mind and your heart working together to produce a great spiritual awakening in you.

Just to be sure you know what your 3rd eye is capable of, look at what happens when your third eye opens:

- Your level of intuition heightens

- Your level of consciousness as well as awareness rises

- You get to have a deeper trust in yourself and also in other people

- You get a better connection with your spiritual guides as well as the universe as a whole

- You get to connect with other people better at a spiritual level

- You are better able to derive answers from your spiritual search and from your surroundings

- You are able to sense and appreciate your energy flow better and to interpret it more appropriately

- Your ability to process information is much more effective as it goes beyond the normal analysis and rational thinking.

What exactly happens in a distinct way when your 3rd Eye opens?

Well, something indisputable happens in heightening your intuition, and this is after having the following experience:

- Some slight stirring, or pressure of sorts, at the location between your eyebrows

- A feeling of inner sigh; some satisfaction of sorts

- You may, sometimes, visualize that third eye opening; or even sense it. People have been known to experience a pop sound in the location of their third eye

- Having some unique feeling when meditating or doing some other visualizing exercises

How does opening your third eye manifest in your day-to-day life?

You surely cannot have your third eye open and be the same person who picks a fight with Tom, Dick and Harry any hour of the day. It is not possible because for you to have that high intuitive ability, you have got to have a clear mind and a positive predisposition. That way, your spiritual energy flows nicely and effectively. Here, then, are other additions that back up your position as a spiritually intuitive person:

- You begin having a fresh outlook to things and situations

- You are now able to accept other people with better understanding, however they are; and even in a more compassionate way

- You have this feeling of being in harmony with the universe

- You feel a spiritual connection with the Divine

- You feel light in spirit and you also have a feeling of tranquillity

- You are able to look at issues in different dimensions

- You are able to make astral travels with relative ease

At the end of the day, what benefits do you reap?

- You are in a better position to make helpful decisions faster and with more confidence

- You have a well from where to tap important information that affects your situation in matters of finance; health; career; and so on.

- You have stronger power to sharpen your skills; abilities; and talents.

- If you are one of those people who help others in a holistic way or in ways that use energy flow, your abilities are better strengthened.

- On the overall, there is a richness that fills your life as you even feel a deeper understanding of yourself as well as being at peace with yourself.

Chapter 31:
How the Master Chakra Works in Summary – The 3rd Eye

Your third eye, as you now know, is the one that controls your thought process up to the point of translating your thoughts into action. It is, therefore, your life's driver, the chakra with the pivotal role of influencing the rest of the chakras. Referring to it as the master is hence befitting. In fact, in Sanskrit where you get *ajna*, a common term for the third eye, the word *ajna* literally means *command*. No wonder major key life drivers have some relation with this sixth chakra – wisdom; intuition; imagination; and even psychic abilities.

If you think about the reality of life, what you visualize for yourself is actually the version of life that you tend to create. If, for instance, you are all fearful, worrisome and anxious, that is what you manifest in life.

Here is distinctly what your third eye governs:

Intuition; psychic abilities; clairvoyance; willpower; higher consciousness; insight; discernment of a spiritual nature; Divine experiences; circadian rhythm or the biological clock; telepathy; awareness; and distribution of Prana or spiritual energy to different areas of your body. As far as your physical body is concerned, your third eye governs your eyes; the pineal gland; and even that bottom part of your brain that is the third ventricle.

How do you tell when your third eye is not in good shape?

When your third eye is not operating as it should, all other chakras are negatively impacted, because as already mentioned, your third eye has significant influence over the way energy flows within those other chakras.

Here are telltale signs:

- Manifesting closed mindedness

- Being egotistic

- Suffering glaucoma

- Suffering cataracts

- Experiencing blurry vision and general poor eyesight

- Having distortions in your perception

- Suffering astigmatism

- Having acute sleep disorders which may include insomnia

- Being too rigid in your thinking

- Having racing incessant thoughts

- Experiencing diminishing confidence in your personal intuition

- Being fearful of your personal intuition

- Suffering unexplained headaches, which may include migraines

- Being a planner and never implementing your ideas; forever procrastinating

- Dangerously acting on impulse

- Suffering hallucinations

- Being very forgetful

- Inability to recall significant dreams

- Suffering low level of imagination; having difficulties grasping the abstract

- Being consistently illogical

- Falling short in spiritual consciousness

- Having low level of intuition and lacking in insight

- Acting in ways that are outright unwise

- Being extremely skeptical about almost everything

- Suffering significant fear in matters relating to life as well as death

- Experiencing fear in matters relating to both success as well as failure

- Being too anxious that you might be wrong

- Experiencing fear in almost everything you deem important – like the Divine; the truth; reality regarding yourself; and consequences of anything you partake in.

- Being too much absorbed by matters of the physical including acquisition of property

- Having trouble telling time, including what day of the week it is

- Having too little faith in most things and most people to the extent of only believing in what you see

- Having doubts about the Divine power

- Consistently lacking in foresight

- Leaning too much on co-dependency

- Being unable to manifest your desires confidently and appropriately

- Being consistently pessimistic to the extent of becoming a perennial non-starter as far as your plans go; being a consistent worrier

- Avoiding to face reality and consistently behaving like the proverbial ostrich – burying your head in the sand

- Being incapable of identifying the good things in a situation and enjoying them; being instead overwhelmed by the bad things irrespective of their magnitude

- Fearing and detesting the gift of intuition instead of embracing it and utilizing it for your good and those of others

Obviously, you cannot help being concerned when you can tell your third eye is doing badly yet you know how important it is to have it working well.

So, How Can You Bring Back The Balance Of Your Third Eye?

Regaining the balance of your third eye so that you are back to being the highly intuitive imaginative and sensitive person you normally are, is not so hard once you know how to go about it.

Here is how to reinstate your third eye:

- Begin visualizing or even dressing in Indigo

- Do some meditation as you visualize an Indigo ball

- Have sessions of listening to music with musical note A. That note, A, is always associated with the sixth chakra

- Having constant sessions of meditation and prayer

- Using tiger balm by rubbing some onto the space of your sixth chakra between your eyebrows. Camphor is a great alternative to tiger balm.

- Using Star of Bethlehem Bach Flower by smearing a drop of it on the space of your sixth chakra between your eyebrows

- Staring at something with full focus, whether living or not, with strong intention of visualizing some light surrounding it.

- Looking into your mirror and staring right into your eyes

- Trusting your own intuition and believing in what it tells you, including visions that you may see.

- Acknowledging your personal fears and then setting out to clear them using the relevant chakras. If necessary, you could consult a psychic to help you clear those fears that are plaguing you.

- Trying to communicate spiritually with other people. For instance, you could do some guessing exercises with someone you are close to, where you guess what they are thinking and they acknowledge it or deny it; then you can tell how well you are doing with your intuition. You could also send images to each other, just mentally.

- Keeping a dream journal where you note down the details of your dream when you awake.

Chapter 32:
Signs That You Have Attained Spiritual Awakening

Did you know that you are not just part of the universe but that you are somehow connected to everything around you? And, of course, it is possible to explain that position when you consider that everything in the universe has energy vibrations within it. Yes – that is true, whether the thing has life as you know it or not. In fact, you may have clicked that from earlier chapters when you observed how crystals, which are mere rocks, and for sure, inanimate objects, work on your system to get you to a better place emotionally and spiritually.

So, yes, you and everything in this universe have something important in common; something central to your state of existence – all energy related. In short, that familiar disparity between animate and inanimate beings is not that final. However, you are only able to appreciate this fact when you have developed the ability to know yourself well at all levels; actually to the level of your soul. That is the time you can aptly declare you have been spiritually awakened and that is because you do not just understand yourself, others and the surroundings, but you also have a deep divine connection.

At this point, you are confident that you can reach to higher spiritual powers for guidance and assistance when you cannot find a way out in the physical world.

The question now is how to tell that you are actually getting spiritually awakened. For that position, you are the only person who can reach that conclusion with confidence. This is because when spiritual awakening is happening within you, there are some things that change and you feel it. Beyond those sensations of your brow that come in at the very initial stages of opening your third eye, there is a tendency for you to have different feelings towards certain things. For example, where you would have lost your temper in provocation, you now respond with different emotions. That is because your attitude towards life and everyone and everything in it changes once you have been spiritually awakened.

And it is not just your emotional feelings that change but all your body patterns in general – physical; mental; and even spiritual. In fact, long before certain big things have happened in your life, you can intuitively tell that you have changed in totality. This is simply because the level of your spiritual energy has risen and your vibrations are now much higher. You even feel much lighter now.

Here are telltale signs that you are spiritually awakened:

Your head either itching or aching

As you get spiritually awakened, you could suffer some slight headache and if not a headache, some sensation within your head area definitely does happen, for example:

- A tingling sensation

- A prickly feeling

- Feeling like minute things are crawling on your scalp

- Feeling like minute things are crawling along your neck from the direction of the head

- Feeling like minute things are crawling along your spine from the top

What you need to take away from this message is that these are not sensations for a dermatologist to deal with. Neither is it time for you to go experimenting with the best advertized moisturizing cream. No – yours, at least this time, is not a case of dandruff or unkempt head. You are simply going through that significant phase of spiritual awakening and it is showing. Is this sensation going to last forever, you may wonder? No – it mainly comes when the door of your third eye is finally going ajar; then it fades away and leaves you confident in your spiritual awareness.

Changing sleep patterns

Do not fret about waking up at 3am or thereabouts when you have not set an alarm for that. And do not worry that your sleep seems to be evaporating after only a few hours of lying down; actually much fewer than you normally have. This is a normal development when your spiritual awakening is taking place. And if you are keen, you will notice that sleeping just those few hours is not affecting your normal day in any adverse manner. It does not and that is because the reason for which you are sleeping so little is healthy. It is the fact that during this time, you are tapping into the divine periodically and this has a way of disrupting your sleep patterns. With that information, you have no reason not to go with the flow.

Also related with your changing sleep pattern is the possibility of experiencing hot flashes or even cold sweats at any time of day or even night. This is just the result of your body trying to adjust to its new energy level. And just like the itching of your scalp, these ups and downs in body temperature also cease after sometime.

Having odd dreams

You may take dreaming to be normal, and it may be to a great extent, but when you find yourself in a dream state and you have been trying to open your third eye, it is usually a sign that you are finally experiencing the spiritual awakening you have been seeking. In fact, you may find yourself in a dream state even when you really are not having much sleep. It is advisable to try and understand those dreams or what they denote because they usually have something to do with your real life, or they are passing on an important message to you – possibly related to an issue you need to take care of.

Hearing a ringing in your ear

This hearing is clearly distinct. And sometimes it is actually not a ringing but a buzzing of sorts. Other times you just feel some unmistakable pressure within your ear. This really happens because the spiritual energy vibrations within you are rising. Yes, the energy flow has been there all along, only it has not been audible. But now that the vibrations are rising in frequency, they create an audible sound which you can literally hear with your physical ears.

NB:

- When the ringing pitch is somewhat low, that is a sign that your spirit guides are around and trying to communicate to you.

- When the ringing pitch is somewhat high, it is a sign that your guiding angels are around and trying to communicate to you.

Now that you know that the temporary ringing or buzzing is not a sign of ill health but rather a sign of positive spiritual development, and since you can now appreciate the presence of your spirit guides and angels, be confident to speak to those higher beings when you hear the sounds. Let them know by verbalizing it that you acknowledge their presence and that you are grateful to them. That acknowledgment is likely to cause the ringing or buzzing to stop faster than it would otherwise have.

Experiencing general body changes

During this life changing period of spiritual awakening, different parts of your body are likely to be variously affected – some with aches, others with sensations of this or that kind, and others just experiencing some tension. Reading informative material such as which you find in this book helps you not to panic.

Here are some physical changes you may register:

- Sporadic aches in particular parts of your body and sometimes in your entire body in general

- Soreness of muscles and sometimes bones

- Feeling of stiffness in your joints

- Soreness within your neck

- Aches in your shoulders

- Pains within your head

What you need to understand is that these aches, pains, soreness and stiffness, which sometimes are coupled with sensations of sorts, are part of what you feel when you are experiencing serious spiritual awakening. However, the

195

assumption here is that you have no injury – physical or otherwise – that may have occasioned your aches; and that you have not been experiencing fatigue of sorts that could occasion such feelings. You need to know too that no caveat has been put against you seeking some chiropractic adjustments, just in case you find the aches and pains too discomforting.

Changes in your vision as well as perception

Ordinarily your range of vision covers the area 180° forwards, and so if that changes there is no way you will fail to notice. In times of spiritual awakening, you can see some dark shadows within your limited peripheral vision. And sometimes what you see in those angles are light flashes or even some sparkles.

Alert: Dark shadows appearing from your peripheral vision are not signs of anything scary; as in nothing related to evil. The shadows may be grey or dark, and sometimes they may even appear gritty. But guess what? They are often just your spirit guides.

Other visual changes:

- Your eyes may turn a little dry

- The eyes may become a little itchy

- Your vision may become periodically somewhat blurry

- Sometimes you may see haze before you

- Sometimes you may even see energy within the air that happens to be static-like

- You could also be seeing people's auras around them

- You could be seeing light surrounding people; animals around you; or even objects.

Do not lose sight of the fact that auras are all energy and so when you are seeing energy, it is a positive development as far as your third eye is concerned.

And as far as your heart is concerned:

- You may experience some fluttering at some point or other

- You may experience some palpitations of a spontaneous nature

- You may notice some energy surge around your heart

- You may experience some strange sensations in the area surrounding your heart as well as your chest

- You may even experience some heaviness within the area of your chest

The question is: do you run to the Emergency Room when you feel some of these energy related sensations around your heart and chest?

Well, you really do not have to rush to the ER unless you have any other related condition. Here you can just bear down; take a cough or two; and that should be it as far as getting your heart back its regular rhythm is concerned. When all those rather strange sensations are taking place around your heart and chest, there is really nothing worrisome happening. It is just your heart chakra doing the opening that is needed for a spiritually awakened individual.

It is just like when your crown chakra is opening – and it does open too during this period of spiritual awakening. You feel:

- Strange sensations in your head

- Strange sensations around your eyes

- Pinpricks in areas of the head close to the crown chakra

- Energy surges that feel warm and sometimes like electric shocks

- Sporadic tingling sensation

- Some unexplained spasms

For some people, opening of the crown chakra comes with more than the symptoms already mentioned. Some symptoms manifest themselves on the skin including:

- Beginning to itch for no good reason on random parts of the body

- You develop acne or even hives in random bouts

- You notice your face is flushing

- You notice your skin developing rashes or other unfamiliar changes

And could you believe your hair, too, bears some symptoms of your spiritual awakening? And your nails as well as you will see below:

- You hair texture may appear to be adversely affected

- Even your hair color may also begin to change somewhat

- You may also notice your hair thinning out

- Even then, there may be some positive signs, including your hair and also your nails growing much faster than ordinarily.

Experiencing some emotional rollercoaster

For the initial stages of spiritual awakening, you are going to lose your emotional stability as you know it, as your energy levels are going to change in an unfamiliar way, and you are going to begin to be conscious of things you were never aware of. And considering that spiritual awakening comes with increased emotional empathy, it should not be surprising that you should experience emotional rollercoaster.

But what, exactly, does it feel to be on an emotional rollercoaster?

- You begin to experienced unexplained periods of nervousness

- You begin to develop unexplained anxiety

- You begin to worry unnecessarily

- You can even begin to experience panic attacks

- You start to feel like you are getting drained of energy when you are in the presence of particular people

- You feel energy drained also within certain environments

- You get that feeling of overwhelm

- You could sometimes feel like you are going crazy, in fact to the level of having a nervous breakdown

Does that list worry you – all the emotions that take you through a rollercoaster ride? You need not worry. This is normal and is not long lasting. In fact, those rather negative symptoms are a result of good things happening underneath.

And can any good come out of emotional upheavals?

Temporal ones like these related to spiritual awakening – yes. You are one person whose awareness has been limited to a great extent and for a long time. And your level of empathy towards other people may not have been that pronounced. All the while, that limitation meant that you were shielded, in a way, from reality. And where you were not shielded, you never allowed yourself to acknowledge some very sensitive issues because you did not want to take charge of the situation.

In short, your system has borne lots of unexpressed emotions for long and now that you are spiritually aware, it is opening up to reality. So, unconsciously, your pent up emotions are showing up and your system is trying to deal with them. This is as it should be because once you acknowledge how you really feel, you can then embark on dealing with the reasons for feeling that way. And before you know it, you have found a way to be emotionally stable, highly intuitive; spiritually aware; and confident in whom you are.

Suffering digestion problems and even positive food cravings

What do you think is happening to your energy vibrations as you become spiritually aware? Of course, they are getting to a higher level. That in itself makes you intolerant to foods that have lower vibrations.

Such foods include:

- Foods containing preservatives

- Foods that have additives

- Foods that contain some form of lactose

- Various pork products

Would you worry about that? Of course, not! Not if you are aware what is good for your health. So when your stomach gets upset 20 minutes into your eating, you need to review the contents of your meal and know what to leave out next time.

And what foods do you crave during spiritual awakening?

Gladly, the foods that you crave are those that would make your doctor celebrate. And they include vegetables as well as salads.

How odd! Most people under different circumstances are known to crave sugars. This kind of craving is truly not the most common, but it is a sign of your body claiming to be taken care of. Your body tends to reject foods that become a burden later. That is why you will be fine with your digestion as long as you are eating organic and natural foods in general. In the meantime, your body is undergoing its own detoxification with its newly found vibration level, and you may experience some unpleasant symptoms because of that.

Such symptoms include:

- A tendency to have some weight gain

- Fluctuating levels of appetite

- Getting extremely hungry and other times thirsty without obvious justification

- Having symptoms like those of someone with flu

All these symptoms manifest even when you have not altered your lifestyle. It may appear strange how you get to add unexplained weight, but this is actually a way for your body to buffer stock against your new energy surge. The reason you need not worry is that this is a temporal phase and within a short while, after your body has gotten comfortable in its new freshness of emotions and stability of energy vibrations, your gained weight will shed. In short, you are having unpleasant symptoms during your natural body detoxification but getting yourself ready for a healthy life ahead – incorporating your physical body; your mind; as well as your soul.

Other things that signal your spiritual awakening include developing a special bond with young children and animals as well; an inclination to having your own space away from the public; high intolerance to negativity; being kind of clumsy more frequently; not coping up with the natural movement of time – finding it moving too fast and other times too slowly; experiencing increased psychic abilities; and above all, experiencing an intense Divine connection.

Chapter 33:
Demystifying The Myths Touching On The 3rd Eye

Have you realized that anything that does not come in black and white often elicits mythical explanations from curious people who know not how to get around to establishing the truth? It happens in everyday life too.

Like once upon a time the Greeks were fascinated by the regular rising of the sun, day in day out, and had to come up with an explanation for that pattern. According to them, their deity, Apollo, who happened to be son to Zeus, the Greek supreme god, rode daily through the skies on a horse driven chariot and brought light to this world. And those horses in charge of pulling the chariot were said to be fiery (just in case someone tried to hijack them midair, possibly...). Really, is that plausible? Did these people even know the distance from the earth to the sun? Of course, not! In what container was that light carried? Don't ask. That is why it is a myth.

<u>Myths regarding the third eye</u>

We try to open the third eye because ordinarily it is fully closed

It is actually not correct that your third eye is entirely closed sometimes because that is an important energy center that must be working if you are living a normal life. It deals with intuition and while you may not be highly intuitive, you must be able to have some level of intellect to appreciate what is going on around you. So, really, while we speak of opening your third eye, it is to the level of reaching heightened awareness levels – that is, you being spiritually aware beyond the ordinary folk. And even as you advance in age and calcification of the pineal gland continues, your third eye is not going to close in totality. At least there is always some tiny crack there.

You can flip open your third eye in a moment's notice

Forget it. Even with all the great information available, opening your precious third eye is always a process. Of course, it does not have to take you years or months, but truth be told, it requires some level of discipline and some patience. And it calls for your full focus.

Anyway, you have already seen that even from simple exercises of meditation. In any case, it is for your benefit that your third eye opens gradually or even after you are psychologically prepared, otherwise the whole experience might be overwhelming for you. Of course you can hide in a cave or other secluded place and hasten the opening of your third eye, but is that usual tendency? No – it is just normal for monks and such other spiritual masters.

The third eye is nothing like the conventional eye

Well, they have similarities. Do your physical eyes deal with light? Sure, they do. And so does the third eye. Do they have lenses? Do they have corneas? Do they have retinas? Yes, each of your physical eyes has a lens; the cornea; and also the retina. Those are parts that your third eye also has. In short, the third eye is not something imaginary though you may not see its energies with your naked eyes, and it does have similarities with your physical eye.

Everyone has similar third eye experiences

Of course, that is a farce. Do you even see the same things as everyone else with your physical eyes? In reality, you see what you focus on, otherwise there is too much to see on your 180° expanse before you that you just cannot take it all in. Similarly, when it comes to your third eye, you could simply become more aware of your surroundings and more empathetic, while someone else could go out on astral travels. Each individual is different in energy vibrations and everything else about our make-up, and so every person has their personalized experience.

Everything about your third eye reeks of evil

There is no truth in that. Just because you are more aware than the average person does not make your abilities evil. Are there no good spirits giving guidance to ordinary mortals? There you have it! The Divine has the strength to communicate with you and anyone else in ways that are not as conventional as common speech. Yet that spiritual communication enables you to bring harmony in ordinary life.

Conclusion

Now that you understand what the Third Eye is, you can start using it every day. Start by ensuring it is open in the first place. Follow the simple steps indicated in this book and watch your life change for the better. With increased awareness about your life in relation to those around you, you will feel confident undertaking certain projects and engaging with different people. This is mostly because the intuitive power of your third eye is able to warn you when certain moves are likely to lead you to danger and when certain others would be fruitful. When you practice opening and closing your third eye, be sure you are getting full control of your life, which is a good feeling and also a good thing for practical purposes.

You may also wish to put your learned skills and enhanced level of spiritual awareness to practice, and see if you can help other people. This is something you can certainly do if you realize you have stepped into the realm of real psychics or even mediums. You may also be useful to parents of children with heightened psychic awareness, so that both the parents and the children can be able to lead normal lives without feeling overwhelmed.

The next step is to go back over the book as needed while you begin to do your routine practices which are bent on enhancing the clarity of your third eye. Certain practices that you do before you go to bed ensure that you have a nice, peaceful sleep, while others that you do first thing when you get up in the morning ensure you begin your day feeling energized and positive about life. Once you have managed to open your third eye, it is unlikely you will wish to ignore it again considering how great you feel when you have the feeling of being in-charge of your life. With your high intuitive power, for instance, nothing really gets you entirely unaware – at least some vibe will have warned you of the possibilities; the power of the third eye.

Reach for the intuitive level you deserve and don't forget to congratulate yourself for a job well done when you finally have your intuitive awareness!

BONUS

ASTRAL PROJECTION MASTERY

Powerful Astral Projection And Astral Travel Techniques To Expand Your Consciousness Beyond The Psychical !

L. Jordan

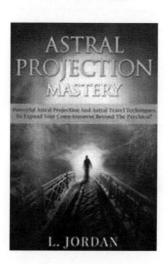

2nd Edition

Free bonus inside this book

Table of Contents

Introduction

Chances are that you have heard of Astral Projection. But the kind of astral projection many people have in mind is one where you see those unreachable glittering spots in the solar system – the stars. Yes, you will see the shining stars if you project your eyes upwards; but that is not what we are about today. Today is about astral projection that allows you to leave your body when you are still breathing and 100% fine. You depart from your physical body and tour another world where nothing can be touched with physical hands despite being clearly seen. Even *you* cannot be touched or harmed once in this realm.

In short, you will learn from this book that you exist on different planes and for that matter your life does not come to an end when your physical body ceases to exist. You can ascertain that through astral projection because you will be able to leave your body and meet other beings that are not physical but spiritual; the same way you are when you enter the astral plane.

This book also points out cases showing that astral projection is gaining credence even among scientists. Much as they rely on physical observation and quantification of results, experiences among fellow scientists have renewed interest in exploring this area of study, with a view to establishing the reality of life on other planes other than the physical.

This book introduces to you simple techniques that prepare you for astral travel; techniques that make projection into the spiritual world one enjoyable experience that is free of fear. You will be amazed that you can do what mystics have always done like it was magic! Go on – pick on a technique of your choice; or better still, try them all, and see which one best suits you. Happy reading and all the best in trying out the techniques of astral projection!

Chapter 1:
What, Exactly, Is Astral Projection?

Do you know of terminologies that are not easily described in a couple of words yet you will not term them as complex as rocket science? Well, astral projection is one of them. For starters, the most direct definition of it is an out-of-body experience – commonly termed OBE. And of course, when you hear of the word *experience* you get to understand why the definition for astral projection cannot be done in a simplistic manner. Experiences can be detailed and varied even for people in the same environment.

The experience alluded to here is your and my experience – the experience of each individual when it comes to visualizing yourself from a different perspective; a viewpoint that is not ordinary as you are not in a bodily state at the time of observing yourself. In short, you are another being that you cannot touch at all, and looking at your bodily self lying down or busy doing other things. It is like you are in wonderland – remember Alice in Wonderland? So you are a liberal non-physical being, traversing wherever you want, without the inhibition of walls, doors, streams, anything physical. Now, could this be your spirit hovering about after you are dead? Oh, no, it is not! Fear not – you are still alive and breathing.

Granted, you are in a spiritual state – only you have not yet given up your physical body. Remember you can see yourself walking the earth like every other being occupying the busy rugged world. You are essentially an observer of the world you are a part of, only this time you have your double in another form – a spiritual form.

And are you sure this astral projection is not a dream? Sure, it isn't – you need to doze off to dream, something you do not need to do to get into astral projection. In fact, with the right skills, you can induce that state of astral projection at any time any place. And it is nothing like popping a sleeping pill or some tots of high alcohol concentration – just some simple consummate focusing.

Simple image of Astral Projection

Just in case you find your abstract mind getting a little muddled up with the explanation already given, let us try to crystallize the image. You have your physical body – yes that is tangibly real – and your spiritual body – that too is easy to appreciate because it is simply your subtle body. Now where you may get lost is the double existence; being in your body, yet having an out-of-body experience. And here is where we bring in the link commonly termed the umbilical cord, to get your physical and your subtle bodies to co-exist and communicate even as they part ways. Sorry, but is this like the child's umbilical cord? Well – something like that. In fact, visualize it that way for a vivid picture. However, your umbilical cord here is not made of flesh and it is not internally tying you to a fetus. It is made of energy – strong energy stream from your chakras, your physical energy points; and it is tying your physical form to your subtle form. Aha! Great – but then you have more than one chakra; more than one energy point. How does that work? Sure, that explanation is vital – you cannot afford to complicate the image that is just about to crystallize.

Luckily, you do not get to see the seven chakras in your body scramble for participation. Ordinarily, many people see this umbilical cord as coming from the navel where the conventional umbilical cord emanates from; and that is fine.

In any case, just to refresh your mind (or to inform you), the chakra at your navel is the one that contains all the energy relating to extraordinary passions like dreams and fantasies. In fact, it is said to provide a strong bond between you and people that you love. And you know in your astral projection that is usually the category of people that you get to visit. However, there is no rigidity when it comes to the location where the energy streams emanate from.

Some people see the umbilical cord as coming directly from the forehead to your subtle body. The reason you will not wish to fault this premise is that the forehead hosts the chakra in charge of imagination, intuition, and understanding of a higher force beyond our simple selves. So, yes – coming from there, the cord cannot be anything but strong in terms of helping the process of astral projection.

Anyway, just to be alive to reality, you could have your astral projection when your navel chakra is not at its strongest and the forehead chakra is just in a lull. What happens then is that your umbilical cord, which in metaphysics is dubbed the silver cord, comes directly from the chakra that is strongest at the time and links your physical body to your subtle body. Even the sacral chakra is not out of contention – you can have the silver cord coming directly from just a couple of centimeters below your navel from whence flows your sexual energy.

What you are going to realize is that once on your astral plane, everything looks and feels real – you experience things as though you were in the real world, only better. In your astral projection, you see things more broadly than you do in your earthly 220° frontal vision – yeah; you are no chameleon, remember? Yet in your astral projection, you have a whole spherical vision of 360° - at least that is the capability you have. But do you really utilize it? Sometimes no – since you are so used to looking at one direction, of course with limitation of scope, you tend to restrict yourself to that even when you are on the astral plane; and it takes practice to learn to exploit your full capability and learn to experience things comprehensively.

With practice, you get to appreciate the world without the discouragement of an aching body, an aging body or anything else physical. And what does that do to you, guess? It makes you one happy person, with a positive mindset despite any worldly challenges you may encounter. After all, astral projection brings to the fore the fact that there is a higher state of being than the physical. How encouraging!

Chapter 2:
Astral Projection Feels Like A Dream – But Is It?

Astral Projection does really feel like a dream, doesn't it? You being physically immobile and mute, yet you are seeing yourself walking or driving and chatting with people you know in real life... It does really feel like you are dreaming. But are you really in a dream state? The answer is no – dreaming is dreaming and astral projection is what it is. For one, when you are dreaming, you are on the dream plane; but when you are experiencing an astral projection, you are on the astral plane.

You see, in your mind, you have different planes, some higher and some lower than others. Each of the planes is made up of different material or content, and where the content is shared, you have different ways that the stuff is organized on the different planes. On the dream plane, for instance, you can see most of the things that you see on the astral plane. Only when it comes to organization, a dismal job shows up in your dream world. When dreaming, it is not unusual, for example, to find yourself in a ridiculous scenario where you are in a normal High school class, with your mechanic neighbor as your English teacher and the make-up of your class being two of your former elementary school classmates, one former classmate from High school, three from your university, and the rest being strangers. Surely, what can we term this but a random collection of facts and fantasy? And gladly, you know it when you are dreaming. If it was a sweet interesting dream, you wake up thinking – I wish it were true! Remember that all along, no part of you is disentangled – body or spirit.

However, when it comes to astral projection, your spiritual body leaves your physical body and ventures into deep space where there is a link between your mental contemplation and your intellect. In the discipline of theosophy as propagated by experts like Madam Blavatsky of the 1800s, the astral plane is the one that facilitates strong energy from the Prana, which is a higher plane, to seep through to your physical body. This is the exact vitalizing energy that carries you into astral travel. Essentially, you are looking at the astral plane as part of seven acknowledged planes, the lowest being the physical that is the most temporal part of your being; followed in hierarchy by the astral plane, the strong structure around which the physical body exists; and ending with the highest, which is the Atma or Pure eternal spirit.

In fact, you do not have to be deep asleep to shift to the astral plane – you can do it with full consciousness. And it is not similar to a near death experience – no. When you go through a traumatic experience, say, a serious accident, what you do is to lose consciousness and then begin to see things in a remote kind of way. In contrast, as you make your astral travel, you could still be asleep or under anesthesia, or, on the contrary, you could be fully aware of what is happening only in a kind of hypnotic trance. Surely the idea must be forming by now. And you are on the right track if you have begun to imagine having an astral projection while seated or standing in your living room or somewhere familiar for that matter. That is precisely what you are capable of achieving after you have mastered the appropriate skills of traversing the higher realms of existence.

Anything to associate astral projection with the future...?

Question: Would it excite you to know that astral projection can help you have a peek at the future?

Answer: It is actually possible for you to see beyond today through astral projection. They call it astral premonition. And you have to appreciate the import of something big or serious happening when you have prior knowledge of it. Whether it be something good or bad, it does help you to take it in when you have been psychologically prepared than if it catches you unawares. Or have you not heard of people collapsing after receiving overwhelmingly good news just as others collapse of bad news? In any case, who would not like to be forewarned if only to satisfy some curiosity?

Reasons you and others would be interested in astral projection:

- That much talked about curiosity that killed the cat

  You want to experiment and see if you can actually master astral projection, and if so, how far you can go with it. Fair enough – curiosity is part of human nature.

- To interact with other astral beings like spirits of loved ones who are departed

- To allow your physical body to relax

  As you are aware, as long as there is activity of any kind within you, spiritual or otherwise, it will take some energy from your body. As such, any chance for relaxation is more than welcome

- To get some information from that extraordinary spiritual world

- To try and understand the after-life in a better way

- To achieve some healing by releasing any negative energies and tapping into the positive ones.

And just in case it has not yet dawned on you, astral experiences are related to the stars – those bright celestial bodies that bring light and energy into your life, both physical and spiritual. So, no – when you are having a starry projection, you are not dreaming. You are trying to make a brighter life for yourself.